LUNCH & LITERATURE
LEARNING LIFE SKILLS THROUGH LITERATURE

BY MEGAN ANN SCHEIBNER
WITH CHEF EMMA SMOCK

Character Health
101 Casablanca Ct.
Cary, NC 27519

ISBN 978-0-9849714-6-6

Contents

Introducing Chef Emma Smock

Emma Smock began life as Emily Marion Scheibner. She is our third child and second daughter. From her youngest days, Emma loved to cook, experiment, and  generally, make a huge mess in *my* kitchen! After graduation from high school, Emma went on to college where she earned a degree in Culinary Arts, (graduating as Valedictorian of her class) and a second degree in Business. She's one smart cookie!

As I began the revisions of the Recipe and Routine series, it just made sense to involve Emma in the process. Characterhealth.com is truly a family business, with our children involved in every aspect. Choosing Emma to select, develop, and record recipes was an easy decision. It lifted a burden from me, and this time she got to make a mess in her own kitchen! While my recipes are yummy and family friendly, (Emma calls them "Mommy" food) they aren't always nutritionally balanced. There I said it! Sometimes, I cook what tastes good, even if it's not good for you!

Because of Emma's training as a chef and her extensive knowledge of nutrition and meal planning, she provides a great balance to my offerings. Although I gave her incredible editorial freedom, (You're welcome, Emma) I did manage to keep in a couple favorites like Cheeseburger Soup, (Lunch and Literature) and Breakfast Pizza. (Rise and Shine) She held her nose, but allowed me some leeway. Honestly, we don't eat those foods everyday, so I don't feel guilty at all! And, to set the record straight... Cheese curls are really just air, so what's the big deal!

Our family is very healthy with no food allergies, so the recipes you will find use basic ingredients. Please, adapt as necessary to fit your own dietary needs. I did have one daughter who was required to be gluten-free for a time, so I feel your pain. Thankfully, there are more and more substitutionary items to replace the non-gluten free ingredients.

I know you'll enjoy these new revisions and Emma's awesome recipes! I couldn't be prouder of her and working together was a blast... Even when she nagged me about my food choices! Now that she's a mommy, (Thanks for bringing us Oliver, Emma!) perhaps she'll start to eat more like me. Somehow, I doubt it!

> *"I know you'll enjoy these new revisions and Emma's awesome recipes! I couldn't be prouder of her and working together was a blast..."*

www.characterhealth.com

LUNCH AND LITERATURE

Lunch...Ahh that wondrous time when we drop everything we are doing and gather together around a sumptuous meal that has been painstakingly prepared. That delightful moment of the day when everything that so occupies our time and thoughts takes backseat to the relationships and reality of a meal of great importance!

Wait a minute, just whom am I kidding?? I think every busy mother would admit that lunch is that meal that sneaks up on us and attacks us, demanding our attention. For moms of small children, it is often the last hurdle we must cross before our children's naps give us a much-needed respite. For moms of older children, lunch is often an interruption to studies, sports, or free time that proves to be more of an imposition, than a blessing. But, does this have to be how our lunch hour proceeds? Are we destined to simply "put up with" dull, dreary mealtimes? I don't think so! With just the teensiest-tiniest bit of pre-thought and preparation, lunch can become one of your most treasured times of the day. Spending lunch laughing, talking, and sharing memories together isn't an impossible dream, rather it's an easily attainable goal.

Lunch certainly isn't the time to pull out the gourmet ingredients and spend hours preparing tasty tidbits from scratch. (At least not while you have children at home!) However, lunch is a great time to take leftovers and those extra ingredients lurking in your refrigerator to prepare fun and wholesome meals that will recharge your whole family for the rest of the day.

In the same way, the lunch hour is not the time to develop detailed lesson plans for how you are going to use your mealtime to teach life-lessons and address character issues. Oh my goodness, we spend enough time doing that already! Focusing all your attention on those goals will only lead to indigestion for the whole family! Instead, the lunch hour, the time of change from morning to afternoon, is a great time to gather up some simple food and great literature and allow the authors we love to share life lessons and character challenges with our children... without us getting in the way.

Some of my favorite times with my children have been spent around the family table, after lunch and before naps, as we journeyed to other countries and cultures and as we encountered characters that faced the same struggles, temptations, joys, and disappointments, that we faced every day. As my children built relationships with the characters in the books that we devoured, I didn't have to say, "Here is a lesson on honesty, or compassion, or diligence, etc." Instead, they listened as their beloved characters learned those lessons, through good times and bad, right in front of them.

Obviously, there are many other times throughout the day that you will want to incorporate literature into your children's lives, but if you begin with a regular time of lunch hour reading, the results will be quick and impressive. Almost immediately, you will see your children begin to love and desire to be more and more immersed in the inviting community of literary characters. While I will be sharing bedtime and school time and morning reading time ideas, if you are not actively reading to your children yet, let me challenge you to commit to launching a "Lunch Hour Literary Club." I can virtually guarantee that you and your children will love the time and togetherness. Perhaps your biggest problem will become limiting your time to an hour!! Start with a book that you are already familiar with and begin now to incorporate voices and hand motions to help to add personality to the characters in your chosen book. Reading aloud is one of the few times I can really "ham" it up with my children without them thinking that mom is totally off her rocker!

Different families will find different ways to incorporate this Lunch Hour Literary Club. For families who have chosen homeschooling as their educational route, reading together at lunchtime will be easily implemented without throwing off the daily routine. But what about those families whose children are gone over the lunch hour? Obviously, any time you choose to read is a great time, but what about establishing a weekend reading routine. Saturday during lunch or Sunday after the family meal would be a great time to begin a new family habit. For busy, on-the-go, families a predictable time of sitting down, snuggling in, and opening a book together can provide the grounding and security that our families so desperately need.

Now, to be completely honest, I must admit to you that sometimes our leisurely lunch consists of nothing more than peanut butter and jelly sandwiches, with apple slices for dessert. That's okay! However, with just a little creativity, our lunches can be nutritious, delicious, and fun to eat, as well. I will be sharing with you some of our favorite "bar" lunches, simple pizza and stuffed bread recipes, as well as some recipes for soups and homemade breads that are a little more complicated, but when you have the time to make them, they are always a special treat. As a bonus, the final chapter of recipes includes some of our favorite Tea Time recipes.

I know that for many moms of young children, just the thought of trying to corral your children to listen to stories over the lunch table may seem overwhelming. Don't give up, yet! Rather than stretch your little one's morning even later, I would suggest starting your lunch routine earlier.

This alone may curtail some of the late morning grumpiness. Start with short books and build from there. The discipline and delight of shared literature is well worth the short training time involved in teaching your youngest children to participate. As your youngest children begin to engage with you and the older children in the books you choose, you'll see them quickly develop longer attention spans and a greater capacity to be involved and interactive with the stories.

Certainly, as you're gathering your children to read, include books for the youngest children. Don't assume the older children will be bored or uninterested in the books you choose for the little children. Some of my older children are even more intent on making sure I don't skip any pages, actions, or silly sounds that accompany the younger children's books. Those early easy reader books have become beloved friends over the years and the older children welcome hearing them over and over. One of the sweetest things to witness is seeing an older child read aloud a favorite childhood story to their younger sibling, complete with all of "Mom's" crazy sound effects! However, if you have older children as well, I would encourage you to include the little ones in listening to longer and more complex chapter books. You will be amazed at the details and concepts they learn, even before they are able to articulate those thoughts. As well, watching their older siblings eagerly anticipating the lunchtime readings will build a positive peer atmosphere of love for and delight in great literature.

As your older children become proficient readers themselves, teach them how to read aloud with excitement and animation. Your younger children will cherish the time they spend hearing stories read aloud by their older siblings. Often, my older children added a new life and vitality to books that were already old friends to my younger crew. If your older children are reluctant to read aloud, don't allow them the luxury of choosing not to participate. Instead, encourage them to pick a short book and to practice their read aloud skills on a willing sibling. Teach your younger children to express appreciation and gratitude when their older brothers and sisters take the time to read aloud to them. The expressed thankfulness of a younger child will encourage an older, yet reluctant reader to keep on practicing and perfecting their read aloud repertoire.

One of the best things I did for my older children was to send them to a dramatic reading class at our local library. The librarians and some local theatrical performers spent four weeks teaching the children how to "slip into character," in order to turn book characters into real-life characters. This skill has been of great help to my daughters as they began to care for friend's children. A well-read book can often bring calm to a chaotic babysitting adventure. As a part of the girls' "Babysitter's Bag," my girls would include age-appropriate books to be shared with their young charges. Although reading dramatically comes more easily for some of my children than others, they all have learned the basic skills necessary to make reading to others enjoyable. Regardless of what they end up doing in their careers, all of my children will have children of their own, or nieces and nephews, with whom they can share the delight of a well-read story.

On a side note, take the time to get to know your public library and the librarians working there. Most of the librarians that I have had the privilege to know in a personal way, work at the library because they love books and good literature. As well, they love to share their knowledge of good books with interested young readers. Granted, some of their recommendations may not align with your family's personal standards and just because a book is recommended does *not* mean that we need to read that book. Kindly thank the librarian for their recommendation, while just not checking out those books. However, certainly do take the time to utilize the great resource these librarians represent. They have access and knowledge of wonderful books that we might never stumble upon in our visits to the library. Just as a reminder, the librarians that are the most involved with your children will always appreciate thank you notes or little tokens of appreciation! It is important that our children recognize that the librarians are not their personal "book providers," but rather, dear folks who serve the children because they want to see them grow and develop. Some of the librarians with whom we have built strong relationships have actually called our home to recommend books they encounter that they think would be of interest to our children.

Many libraries offer pre-school story hours. We have always taken advantage of these sweet opportunities. For me, listening to the librarians read aloud to the children provided great training in how to capture a child's attention. I listened closely to their inflection and tone. For my children, they were often introduced to new books that soon became beloved friends. The crafts and songs that the librarians incorporated into story hour became a part of our family history. Occasionally, the librarian would pick a book that just wasn't appropriate for my kids. I didn't make a fuss about the book choice. Instead, I quietly led my children from the room and began picking out our weekly stash of take-home books. No librarian is going to please every mom, every time! Because we always took the time to verbalize our gratitude and often sent small gifts, the librarians never took offense when we left the room. They knew they were appreciated and they trusted me to make wise decisions for my own family.

Some moms may be uncomfortable with the idea of reading aloud to their children. My best advice to you is this... practice, practice, and practice again! If you are really uncertain how to go about reading to your children, check out some unabridged story tapes at your library and play them for your children, as you listen along. Listen to how great storytellers use their voices to added personality to each of the characters. Observe the reader's tone, tempo, and pace. However, while story tapes are a great temporary help, don't depend on them for too long. Hearing their own mom read stories to them will build memories for our children that no taped storyteller could ever replicate.

Let me add one disclaimer to that last paragraph. If you really want to build a special memory for your children, enlist their grandparents to read some great stories aloud to them and capture it on tape or CD. When my father read stories onto tape for my children, he interjected little personal comments to each child, making the tapes a special and much treasured memento. Don't wait to do this! By the time we began to tape my dad, we only had a few months left with him; how I wish we had begun earlier and included all of the grandparents! (I first wrote this in 2009, since then, technology has grown by leaps and bounds! Now, with my own grandchildren, I can video myself reading on my smart phone and send it to them. Don't miss the opportunity to interact with your children using both classic literature and up-to-date technology!)

Children who are read to are more prone to become readers themselves. Children who have great literature read to them are more prone to imitate the lives and character of their favorite book heroes. Children, who participate with their parents in the love of great literature, will in turn, pass that love of reading on to their own children. What are we waiting for? I can't think of a better family legacy to pass on to our children, grandchildren, and on and on it goes... Let's grab some great literature and begin developing great readers and great kids!

"Children who have great literature read to them are more prone to imitate the lives and character of their favorite book heroes."

www.characterhealth.com

LITERATURE DEFINED

What is great literature, anyway? If you were asked to define what literature encompasses, would you be able to do so? It is, by no means, my intent to come to you as the "expert," who can tell you exactly what books to read and what books to avoid. However, after years of study and the blessing of growing up in a family of voracious readers, with an English teacher as a mother, I want to share with you what I have learned about books in general and classic or "great" books as well.

If you go to your public library and begin to walk through the shelves and shelves of books, you might assume that for a book to make it onto those shelves, it must be literature and worthy of being read. I would strongly disagree! In my college literature studies and in my time as a mother and writer, I have researched hundreds and hundreds, (maybe even thousands,) of books. As I went through bookshelf after bookshelf, I was disheartened by the many books I found inhabiting library and bookstore shelves, that have no inherent excellence or quality to their story lines. In fact, I would argue that many of those books would cause more character decay than character growth in our children's lives. Just because a book is published, does not mean that it is a good choice for your family. Moms, be discerning! Preview all of the books, or at least sections of the books, that your children will be ingesting! It is always easier to avoid the danger found in questionable reading choices, than to try to erase the images that have been implanted in our children's minds. The written word is an incredibly powerful tool. It can stimulate our children's imaginations and emotions and generate memories for years to come. However, poorly chosen books can do the same thing. Those choices can stimulate negative imaginings, stir up premature or ungodly emotions, and generate guilty memories for years to come. Choose carefully! Don't be afraid to say no, not yet, or let me check!

Here is how I would define great literature. Great literature has characters and stories that will impact our hearts and stir up in us virtue and beauty. Great literature does not depend on contrived situations to blatantly teach life lessons, but instead so involves you in the lives of the characters that you, the reader, learn the life lessons right alongside the characters. This is not to say that characters in great literature always make the right decisions or choose the right paths, but great literature teaches, through those bad choices, the consequences that come from heedless and foolish choices. Great literature strengthens and builds our vocabulary and assumes that the reader is bright and interested. Great literature does not "dumb down" the content, but encourages the reader to rise to the challenge. Great literature draws us into the story and causes us to align ourselves with the characters; sharing their joys with them and grieving right alongside them in their sorrows. Great literature inspires!

Characters in great literature become friends to our children. Often, when they are confronted with hard decisions or challenging situations, it is the remembrance of the actions of their favorite characters that will help them to make wise decisions. I know that I would much rather have my children consider the actions of wise" book friends," than the 12 year old on the soccer team, whom everyone thinks is so "cool." Life experiences that mirror the experiences of their "book friends" remind our children that they are normal, and that what they are encountering has been dealt with and lived through before. Great books can help our children deal with disappointment, discouragement, and grief. Great literature can teach our children to rejoice and be excited for the blessings others receive. The list of the benefits found between the covers of great books is beyond measure.

By contrast, too many works of modern literature work in the opposite manner. Instead of inspiring our children to great deeds, great thoughts, and great character, those books encourage our children to take a different path. Often, the books teach our children that it is acceptable, in fact even honorable, to use a little bit of evil to achieve a good end. Be careful of these types of books. According to the Word of God, it is NEVER right to do wrong in order to achieve something good. Imitating fictional characters in this way will lead our children down poorly chosen paths and can even cause them to have to face permanent consequences.

Great literature will become those books that we return to again and again. These books, with their meaningful life stories, become a safe place, a haven of security, for our children. Not only do the characters become dear friends, soon you will begin to see your children assimilate themselves into the story lines. As a young girl, I spent hours wearing a long skirt and pretending I was Jo March, from *Little Women*. What a relief to follow the story of Jo's life and realize that even a tomboy, like me, would be just fine! My brother was equally enthralled with Jim Hawkins, from *Treasure Island,* and he paraded around our house carrying the necessary compass and knife. This kind of play-acting is so healthy and builds great memories and self-confidence in our children. As a teenager, when I longed for someone...anyone... to act in a courageous and heroic way, I would retreat to my

bedroom for days to reread *The Lord of the Rings*.
I struggled along with Frodo through the grey
desolate wasteland of Mount Doom and rejoiced
with all the people groups of Middle Earth at the
crowning of the King. That series of books, more
than any other, helped me as a self-conscious
teenager, to strive to be a person of courage
and character. As an adult, I've certainly enjoyed
the movies based on the books by JRR Tolkien;
however, no movie can ever rival the lessons
learned and relationships built through reading the
books firsthand.

Developing children who love literature is
not a hard task, although it does take time
and commitment. Our children will love and
appreciate those things with which we surround
them. If your home is full of video games and
gaming systems, those are the things your
children will love. If everything in your home is
sports-oriented, your children will see sports as

desirable and important. If you play lovely music and provide instruments for your children to practice playing, they will see music as a priority. None of these occupations are wrong, and our family participates in many of them, but have you put the same importance and diligence into developing children who love and appreciate fine literature? When I was growing up, my home was full to overflowing with wonderful works of literature. My mother and father were avid readers and they passed that love on to us. One of my closest friends lived across the street. Her folks were wonderful people with many interests, but they just weren't interested in reading. Tina found so many excuses just to be in our home. As a child, I didn't really understand why she never wanted us to be at her house; I thought she didn't like her parents. The truth was this: she longed to be surrounded by books. When we were in college, she told me how much she loved just coming into our home and walking the bookshelves reading the titles and touching the leather spines of the books. She found "home" in the shelves of my house and she just couldn't get enough of the books we kept there. Do you love and appreciate great literature? If not, begin today to build your literature-reading muscles and see what joy and growth in character great literature will bring into your home.

Take the time to teach your children to appreciate and care for their books. Books that are thrown on the floor or trampled underfoot will not be held in the same high regard as books that are carefully placed on tables and consistently returned to their proper shelves. I still own many of the classic books that were purchased for me as a young child. As I sit here today, working at my desk, I can see the soft brown covers of my Louisa May Alcott series. I inherited my mom's complete set of Agatha Christie mystery books and they line the shelves in my office. Each week after church, my dad took me to the local bookstore where he purchased the newspaper and bought me a new Nancy Drew book. The bright yellow covers of those books smile at me across the office and evoke sweet memories of time spent with my dad. Both of my parents stressed the importance of taking especial care as I handled my books and so the books are still in good shape today. I have worked hard to teach my children how to be gentle and care for their books, as well, Someday, the books they enjoy will still be enjoyed their children and my grandchildren.

Books make wonderful gifts! Toys may wear out and clothes will be outgrown, but books are an investment in the future. A beautifully illustrated book with a simple note encouraging the reader will be a long-term gift that brings back special memories and cements your relationship. When purchasing gifts for friend's children, consider the books your children love and ask them for their best recommendations. My daughters have "spontaneously" generated their own book clubs as they shared their love of certain books with their friends via phone, email, and in person.

In fact, when friends of ours were ready to buy their first piece of fine furniture, they contacted my husband and asked him to construct for them one of his beautiful bookcases. He made the bookcase to their specifications, with one shelf for each of their children. That Christmas, the family gift was the lovely bookcase and each child received a hard-backed book to place on "their" shelf. Whenever we went to visit our friends, the first thing their children showed us was their bookcase and the new books they were collecting. That one simple act built an atmosphere in their home of delight in reading and anticipation as they determined which book would join the bookshelves next.

In our own family, we limit the number of gifts that we share at Christmas. However, every year the children know that they will receive a new book that is theirs and theirs alone. We encourage the children to lend their special books to their other siblings. However, all of our children know that when they leave our house, those special books will accompany them to their new homes. Interestingly, with eight children, we have eight different tastes in books. So, although they do pass their books back and forth, it isn't difficult to know whose books are whose. Because everyone has such different tastes, as they have shared books they have learned to go beyond what is comfortable or normal for them to read and they have stretched their knowledge and curiosity. My son, Peter, and daughter, Emma, took the book sharing to a whole new level. When they were both in high school, Emma took it upon herself to encourage her brother to dress just a bit more "cool." (I think now my kid's call it "fresh!") She made a deal with her brother. She promised to read 5 books of his choosing if he would allow her to pick out some clothing for him. He also had to agree to wear the clothing she picked out! Some of the books he chose were quite long and detailed. (I.e. The Count of Monte Cristo and Scottish Chiefs) Although Emma allowed herself a fair amount of moaning and groaning, she completed the books and found, to her surprise, that she actually enjoyed them. Peter wasn't so sure about her clothing choices, but we all thought he looked MUCH better!

Moms, make sure that you have some books that belong to you, as well. Children learn as much, if not more, by watching and imitating us as they do by our verbal instruction. Model a love for reading great books and even for reading books that are just for fun. I always allow my children to borrow my books as long as they treat the borrowed books with respect, for example, not bending pages, breaking the bindings, or dropping them in the tub. (Long story, don't ask!) Insist on this careful attitude. Your books will remain in good condition and your children will be learning great habits of careful stewardship toward their own books.

While having lots of great books around the house and teaching your children to be careful with them is a positive start, these actions alone won't make for literature-loving children. The books on our shelves and in our libraries have to be opened and read and re-read to begin to build a life-long and satisfying relationship with the literature found within the pages. In order to find time to open and read and re-read our books, we are going to have to structure reading time into our busy schedules. When we are uber-super-busy and always on the go, reading for enjoyment will be difficult to schedule. Although I kept a basket of books in the car for long car rides and errand running, that "car reading" didn't really build the deep love for literature that I was trying to produce. Think about your day and week. Is there time for relaxed reading? Do your children know that it's okay to simply sit and interact for an extended period of time with the book of their choice? Or, is your schedule so full that they must quickly fit in the prescribed number of pages and then rush off to the next activity. Building character through reading great literature takes time and a commitment to the priority of character-driven reading. Only we can make the choice to free up that time for our children and when we choose not to make the time, we are sending a clear message regarding our feelings toward reading as a priority activity.

No child is too young to begin enjoying great literature. I'm afraid that sometimes we read our smallest children useless and poorly written books simply because we don't think that they can receive any benefit from fine literature. While the occasional "movie book" or "TV character" book isn't completely harmful, how much better to build, from the beginning, a love for books full of complex characters and imagination building vocabulary. If you build, from their earliest days, an appetite for great literature, your children will be drawn to those types of books when they are old enough to make their own decisions about literature and reading choices. Don't be afraid to stretch them beyond what is comfortable. I think you'll be surprised and thrilled to see them rise to the standard of books you provide and begin to love challenging themselves with more difficult books.

Besides reading aloud to your children, as I said before, it's important to incorporate times during the day that they spend time, interacting with books by themselves. Even before my children were old enough to read to themselves, I instituted a "rest hour," during which time they could sit or lie on their beds and read books. Although they could sleep if they needed to, this was not a time for toys and jumping around. For the non-readers, I sent them off with books that I had read to them over and over again. In fact, I'd read the books so many times that they basically knew the stories by heart. Often, these children would proudly "read" me the book they had been looking at during rest hour. For the children who were old enough to read by themselves, I helped them to pick out books according to their personalities and interests. Often, I pushed them to read books that they did not initially think looked interesting. Many times, these books became their favorites. If after fifteen minutes, the book they had chosen just wasn't interesting to them, I allowed them to pick another book. If picking a new book became a daily, every 15-minute habit, I began to re-start their rest hour with every new book choice. Suddenly, they began to stick with books and to keep reading through the not-so-interesting parts!

Let me share some thoughts with you about choosing books for your children to read. Do not force yourself into a mold where the only books you pick for your boys are "boy books," while the usual books you choose for your girls are "girl books." Great works of literature transcend gender and age and are appropriate for both your sons and your daughters. You will be doing your children a terrible disservice if you segregate them from certain books simply because you think the subject matter is too boyish or too girlish. Consider books such as *A Girl of the Limberlost* or *Tom Sawyer*. A decision, based solely on the titles of these books, would be a great loss and your children would miss out on some endearing characters with invaluable lessons to teach concerning honesty, compassion, forgiveness, and much more.

Don't be afraid to encourage your children to attempt to read some books that just seem "too hard" for them. As they become captivated by a great story and involved with winsome characters, your children will begin to challenge themselves to read harder and more challenging books. This transition will happen seamlessly and without prodding or scolding from you; the books will do all the work! As a reminder however, make sure that you are aware of the content of the more difficult books that they are choosing. There is nothing wrong with refusing to allow your child to read a book that you believe is beyond what their maturity and discernment warrants. Plots and storylines that are appropriate for a teenager will often not be appropriate reading for an eleven year-old, regardless of that child's reading skill. Don't allow misplaced pride on your part regarding your child's competent reading skills to cause them exposure to subject matter that is beyond their age, maturity, or ability to emotionally understand.

During rest hour, the occasional book on tape is no problem. However, I would encourage you not to allow your children to make this choice too often. Reading books by themselves can quickly begin to seem too challenging when it is so much easier to simply slip in the tape or CD and let someone else do the hard work of reading for them. This is not the goal; you want to teach them to interact with the books themselves. Besides, what fun is it to curl up with a good CD? I know I'm a bit odd, but I just find great comfort and joy in the soft feel and warm smell of a well-worn book!

Now, with a basic understanding of what encompasses great literature, we can begin to look at how to incorporate literary works into your unique family and situations, the immeasurable benefit of biographies and historical fiction, some dangers to avoid, and finally, some "not-so-great" literature but, really fun books. There are so many great books to choose from and embracing those books will fill your home with fun, memories, and strong lessons of honor, courage, and character.

MAKING THE MOST OF GREAT LITERATURE

Not all books are appropriate for all times and not all books are appropriate for all children. What do I mean by this? It is important, as a mom, to look at your days and determine your goals for the situation in which you find yourself. Are you getting the children ready for bed? Are you beginning the afternoon after a long nap? Are you filling the hours of a tedious car ride? Different literature is right for different times. In the same way, your children's personalities, temperaments, interests, and even sin appetites should play a part in the decision making process of choosing appropriate literature for their consumption.

Let's begin with small children and bedtime literature. As you observe a variety of children's books, you will begin to sense a different mood and atmosphere in each book. Dr. Seuss books, while really fun, will NOT help to calm your children and prepare them for a restful night's sleep. If the last book they hear before retiring for the night is *Hop On Pop*, don't be surprised if you hear some hopping and popping going on in the bedroom! Instead, choose one of the wonderful calming books that have been written for small children. *Good Night Moon*, by Margaret Wise Brown, has been a favorite with my children year after year. Just glancing at this little book, you might miss the beauty of the story, but for small children the repetition and calm and secure atmosphere are exactly the right end to a busy day.

Looking for some other end-of-the-day recommendations? Any book by Margaret Wise Brown is a great choice. Look for titles like *The Runaway Bunny*, *The Little Fur Family*, or *The Little Fisherman*. Many of Russell Hoban's "Frances" books are a simple and sweet way to end your child's day. Another good choice would be books by Robert McCloskey such as *Time of Wonder* or *One Morning in Maine*.

For your small children, find an end-of-the-day book that both of you love and stick with that book. For young children, a large selection of titles is not necessary and instead, is often counter-productive. Children will respond and relate closely with a story that they hear predictably, night after night. This repetition will assist in their bedtime routine and bring security and comfort to the end of their day. Make sure that you tell babysitters the book, or books, that your children are currently enjoying to end their day. This prior instruction to your babysitters will help with any fearful or insecure feelings the children experience while being tucked in by someone other than mom or dad.

In our home, my husband and I each had different bedtime stories we read to the children. There was a great predictability for them, knowing which story they would hear from which parent. Occasionally, I would try to read aloud one of the books that was a "Dad's story." As you can imagine, the children wouldn't fall for that ruse and would request that I stick to my own stories. I must admit, their Father often chose more rousing stories than I would have chosen, but somehow he still managed to get them calmed down and ready for bed. I'm convinced that those types of differences are part of the reason that God gives children a mother AND a father!

When my children were young, I read many articles that strongly asserted that the only way for me, as a Christian mother, to end my children's day appropriately, was by reading Bible stories. Although Bible stories are a fine choice for end of the day reading, there is no inherent magic in choosing to end your day this way. If you decide to end your day with Bible stories, that's great! However, for my children, I found it more beneficial to have our Bible story time during the morning. I did this for a couple of reasons. First, I wanted to establish the habit, from the earliest age, that we needed God to be involved in our day from the very first moment. The best way for us to accomplish this goal was to read Bible stories and spend time fellowshipping with the Lord to start our day. Secondly, I believe that Bible stories are incomplete without a time of discussion to cement in all of our minds, the lessons we just learned. I don't know about you, but when my children were about to go to sleep, the last thing I wanted to do was to get their minds and mouths going with questions that need to be answered immediately. Instead of nighttime Bible reading, I made sure to close their day with prayer to address all of the pressing concerns they had on their hearts.

Allow me to share a thought about Bible reading in general. I have observed many moms and dads that are tremendous readers and storytellers. They use their voices to add personality and inflection to characters and scenes in books, thus bringing the stories to life for their children. Sadly, these same parents often seem to lose that excitement and involvement when reading Bible stories to their children. Their voices become monotone and the stories becomes nothing more than a check in the block... necessary, but unexciting. Don't let this observation characterize you. The Bible is the greatest work of literature ever written and even more importantly, it is TRUE! When we read the scriptures aloud to our children, nothing should be more exciting to us and that excitement should be evident to our children. Hearing us narrate Jesus' Sermon on the Mount or Paul's defense on Mars Hill should stir our children's hearts and souls and draw them closer to God. Our delight in the Word of

God will translate into our children's awe and delight for that same Scripture. Again, if you are insecure in your ability to read aloud with that type of excitement and inflection, go in your room, close the door, stand in front of your mirror, and practice, practice, practice!

Although there are many great Bible storybooks available today, my all-time favorite is still the *Egermeier's Bible Story Book*. This book goes straight through the Bible, from Genesis to Revelation. The stories go into great detail and you will find yourself checking your own Bible, as you discover facts that you never noticed before. As a family, we have journeyed through the Egermeiers more times than I can count and you can be sure that this one book will be a guaranteed gift to my grandchildren-to-be.

Sometimes, you may find yourself at a point in the day when bedtime is still hours away, but you still need to calm down your rambunctious children or change the atmosphere in your home to avert some disciplinary catastrophe. Sometimes, our days just become too busy. As we run our children here and there to play dates, practices, lessons, and appointments, we can begin to lose the sweet simplicity of childhood. Our children need down time to just sit quietly and relax or to fill their time with no set agenda. Peaceful, unhurried books can help to remind both our children and us what this simple uncluttered time looks like. There are many great books available to fill this very need. *The Wind in the Willows,* by Kenneth Grahame, is a sweet story with peaceful illustrations and a relaxed storyline. The *Frog and Toad,* series by Arnold Lobel, will achieve the same purpose. One of my favorite authors of this type of book is Marguerite de Angeli. Her stories are gentle and the illustrations are beautiful. Some titles to look for include: *Thee, Hannah, Henner's Lydia, Copper-Toed Boots,* and *Petite Suzanne.* There are many books of wonderful children's poetry that extol the joys of family, childhood, and simple pleasures. Keep a supply of these books on hand to pull out when the craziness of life is beginning to overwhelm your family.

Another use for great literature is to teach our children what loving families look like and how they should function as a team. There are some great stand-alone books that serve this purpose, but even more beneficial, I believe, are the series' that draw your children into one family's life for an extended period of time. As your children grow, alongside the characters in these beloved books, they will be learning lessons of compassion, patience, humility, self-control, and more. As a starting point, begin with the *Little House on the Prairie* books by Laura Ingalls Wilder. As you work your way through this series of books, you will notice that each book becomes progressively longer and the vocabulary becomes progressively more advanced. Your child will be learning and growing right along with Laura and Mary. Another great series of books is the *All-of-a-Kind Family* books by Sydney Taylor. Not only will your children become engrossed in the lives of the sisters they will meet in this series, they will learn lessons about family unity and the Jewish culture, at the same time. The children in both of these series are not perfect, but the lessons they learn through times of obedience and disobedience, will be beneficial to your children, now and in the future. Providing dress-up clothes for your children to use as they enact the stories they have read will help the lessons go deeper and be more permanently imprinted on your children's hearts.

For younger children, some stand-alone books that teach this family dynamic are: *Make Way For Ducklings* and *Blueberries for Sal*, both by Robert McCloskey. As well, *The Relatives Came*, by Cynthia

Rylant is a hilarious look at extended families and the fun they can enjoy together.

 Older readers will enjoy *The Swiss Family Robison* by Johann Wyss, or any of the excellent books by Louisa May Alcott. Make it a point to have your children read these books prior to watching the popular Disney movies of the same title. In some cases, the story told in the literature is virtually unrecognizable in the movie version. Especially when it comes to strong father figures, the movies tend to turn males into comedic foils, while the books hold up these same fathers as excellent examples of leadership, commitment, and sacrificial love for their families.

Why is it so important to teach our children about family unity? For many of our families, sibling rivalry and peer dependence has become the norm. I don't believe that this was God's plan for us when He placed us in families. I'm afraid that children who have never learned to love their own families will grow up to be adults that find all of their most meaningful relationships outside of their own families. The tribes of people groups found throughout the Scriptures were simply families that had grown and prospered. God put you and your children into your family for a reason and that reason is to bring honor and glory to Him. Children who speak unkindly and disrespectfully to their parents and to their brothers and sisters are painting a negative picture of both their family and God's family.

You will often see the acronym: J-O-Y, used to illustrate the concept of Jesus, Others, Yourself. In our home, I changed the meaning of the letters to stand for Jesus, Our Family, and Your Other Friends. I want my children to learn how to give their best time, care, and friendship to their brothers and sisters. Unfortunately, without careful teaching, our children will save those best efforts for peer friendships... friendships that are often short-lived and unprofitable. Teaching our children, from the beginning, that God chose their brothers and sisters for them and that He desires to see them become close friends, will pay huge dividends. I'm not saying that this teaching is always easy or that you will always see the fruit that you desire, but don't allow sibling rivalry or indifference to family relationships to characterize your family.

Look carefully at how the characters in the books you choose treat the other members of their families. Books like *Ramona the Pest* and *Harriet the Spy*, while they may be good for a laugh, send a message about families in general and little sisters in specific that I wouldn't want to see copied in my own home. These stories END well, but the means of getting to the positive ending employ disrespect and disregard for important family relationships.

Although the "Dick and Jane" books are irrelevant as primers to teach the skill of reading, they have resurfaced as wonderful read-aloud books for families. What is it that makes these simple books so appealing? The Dick and Jane books are shining examples of a family where each member of the family loves and cares deeply for the other family members. Dick and Jane empathize with one another and with their little sister Sally, while Mother and Father are loving and involved. Books like these build a desire in our children to be loving and kind at home, rather than cool and aloof to parents and younger siblings. Once again, these aren't lessons that you have to point out to your children, they will be internalizing these values as they enjoy hearing the stories and when they are old enough, reading the stories for themselves.

So many life lessons can be taught painlessly by using great works of literature. Although I won't share a comprehensive list here, I do want to share some suggestions to get you started on your reading adventure.

Do you want to teach your children how to be courageous? Look to your library for some great books with courageous characters that will teach and encourage your children to be brave and true. For your younger children, read aloud *The Steadfast Tin Soldier*. Your children will be struck by the bravery shown by the life and death of Hans Christian Anderson's character. For new readers, books like *Danger At the Breaker*, by Catherine Welch and *Keep the Lights Burning, Abbie,* by Peter and Connie Roop will allow them to meet courageous characters on their own, without the assistance of mom. A personal favorite of my children has always been *The Courage of Sarah Noble*, by Alice Dalgliesh.

Many, many books have been written for older readers emphasizing characters who are brave

and courageous. A few examples would be
Johnny Tremain, by Esther Forbes, *The Lost Prince*,
by Frances Hodgson Burnett, and *Robinson
Crusoe*, by Daniel Defoe. Once you have found
an author that your children enjoy and with
whom they connect, check the Internet and your
local library for other books written by the same
author. Although there are always exceptions,
I have found that an author who is trustworthy
and inspiring in one book is generally the same in
his/her other books.

Our children may never have to leave our homes
to fight in a war. They may never find themselves
alone on a deserted island. However, everyday
they face opportunities to choose to be brave
and courageous, or to choose to give in to peer
pressure and situational ethics. Introducing our
children to literary characters who exemplify the
highest levels of courage and bravery will help
them to build the moral muscle necessary to

withstand temptation and consistently make good choices; whether we are present, or absent.

One of the most common themes found in children's literature is the theme of perseverance or steadfastness. It is never too early to begin to teach your child this important character quality. Look for books that show characters finishing what they have begun and overcoming difficulties to succeed. From the youngest children to adult readers, you will find this theme repeated, over and over. What a great character quality to instill in our children's lives! Children who are characterized by a stick-to-it attitude are the children that will stand out as leaders in their homes, schools, and churches. Our country is succumbing to a culture of quitters. If a task seems too hard, many just give in and abandon what they have begun. Building relationships with literary characters that persevere through hardships will begin to give our children the tools they need to "keep-on-keeping-on" when the going gets rough.

Let me suggest some books for younger children that you can read aloud to enforce the character quality of perseverance. Again, this list is not comprehensive, but my hope is that you will read these books and begin to develop an eye for other books with the same type of quality and excellence. Eric Carle has developed an extensive line of picture books that teach perseverance and patience. Look for titles such as: *The Very Busy Spider*, *The Very Clumsy Click Beetle*, *The Very Hungry Caterpillar*, *The Very Lonely Firefly*, and *The Very Quiet Cricket*. I especially love the vivid colors and interactive quality of these books. *Mike Mulligan and His Steam Shovel* and *Katy and the Big Snow* are two books by Virginia Lee Burton that give inanimate objects such a strong personality that young children will be rooting for them to succeed. One of the most popular children's books ever written that teaches perseverance is *The Little Engine That Could,* by Watty Piper. If you haven't read this book to your child yet, run to the library today! My children could have listened to this book every day and sometimes it seemed as though we did read it every day.

For your beginning readers, a couple titles to choose from are *Apples To Oregon,* by Deborah Hopkinson and Nancy Carpenter, and *Baby Island,* by Carol Ryrie Brink. At this point, we own only one copy of *Baby Island* and there has been great debate among the children concerning which of them will eventually succeed in owning our beloved copy.

Older readers should have no trouble finding books that encourage perseverance and steadfastness; the problem may be in monitoring the time spent reading! Although the movie National Velvet is entertaining, the book by the same name and authored by Enid Bagnold is inspiring and motivating. Your horse lovers will especially enjoy this book. Other titles encompass books such as: *Hans Brinker and the Silver Skates*, by Mary Mapes Dodge, *Calico Bush*, by Rachel Field, and *Carry On Mr. Bowditch*, by Jean Lee Latham.

Keeping books like the ones that I have recommended available will be a huge help when your children approach you with the dreaded, "I'm bored." All to often, the easiest thing for us to do is to put in a movie or turn on the computer. A basket of books previewed by mom, will open up a whole new vista of cultures, personalities, and ideas, for our children. There is nothing elaborate or difficult about providing these resources for your children, just a commitment to great literature that teaches great lessons.

MAKING THE MOST OF BIOGRAPHIES AND HISTORICAL FICTION

D o you want your children to impact their culture? Do you want your children to dream great dreams and envision heroic futures? Then, invest in a wide selection of high quality, well-written biographies and works of historical fiction for your home library.

Great works of fiction can definitely inspire our children and help to instill the desire for great character into their life... However, even more so, I believe that biographies and historical fiction can take that character for today and turn it into leadership for the future. Because biographies are true stories, our children can see how real people dealt with real-life issues and how those same, often ordinary people, impacted their world and culture.

Good books of historical fiction will achieve this same purpose. I am not talking about the historical romance novels that are simply set in an earlier time period, but real works of literature that recall true events. The best historical fiction is based on accurate accounts of people and events with a few fictional characters added to the stories.

I haven't conducted any statistical analysis, however in my own eight-child test group, I have found some facts to be true about reading biographies and historical fiction. The first truth is this: the amount of time spent watching movies and/or television and the amount of time reading easy books and playing video games, will directly impact our children's interest in biographical literature. When children are immersed in fast-moving, easily ingested, sitcom type pursuits; the deeper, more complex stories and situations of biographies and historical fiction will not hold their attention. Just like green beans or mushrooms, our children must build an appetite for these multi-layered works of literature. Push through your children's resistance to this type of literature and patiently wait for the results.

The second truth follows and is related to the first. Children who are encouraged to stick with it and read biographies and historical fiction will become children who love and desire to read this type of literature. I have found, with all eight of my children, that it took work and lots of verbal encouragement to get them started reading these books. However, once they had completed a couple of books, they began to search out more of the biographical literature on their own. Start early! Although some of the early reader biographies may not be the greatest works of literature that you will ever encounter, the simple facts enclosed in the pages will begin your children down the road to a lifetime enjoyment of biographies and historical fiction.

Another simple introduction to historical fiction are the diary type books published by Scholastic books. Although I wouldn't want to depend on these simply written books for an extended period of time, they can be a nice introduction to historical characters and historical literature. Often, I have used these diary type books to begin a study on an historical character and then sought out further books related to that time period or historical person.

Too often, children will look at biographies or historical books as "schoolish" reading and therefore, something to be avoided. It is our job as parents, to incite an excitement in our children's hearts for the precious literary gems that these books can become. Choosing to read a biography aloud as a family can be a great help in getting your children involved. In addition, using the well-produced *Your Story Hour* tapes as a springboard to further reading on a subject is often a fun way to get your children excited and anticipating getting to know more about an historical character or time in history.

Don't limit yourself to a certain type of biography, but enjoy the wide range of biographical literature available. Do you have a child who loves sports? Look for biographies of sports heroes, past and present. Do you have an inventive child or one who loves to create? Look for biographies of men and women like: Henry Ford, Albert Einstein, Marie Curie, Alfred Nobel, or Wilbur and Orville Wright. For a child with a penchant for writing, find them biographies of such great authors as: Louisa May Alcott, Alfred Lord Tennyson, C.S. Lewis, or J.R.R. Tolkien.

For the Christian, biographies of great heroes and martyrs of the faith will assist in building and equipping our next generation of missionaries, pastors, and outspoken apologists for the Lord

Jesus Christ. As children interact with true stories about Christians such as: Jim Elliot, Nate Saint, Amy Carmichael, Eric Liddell, and so many more, they will begin to understand the scripture found in Philippians 1:26, "For me to live is Christ, and to die is gain." The words and actions of these great believers from the past can serve as the spark to ignite the fire of faith in young believers, our future Christian leaders.

Foxes Book of Martyrs provides a wealth of short biographical stories of the brave Christians whom have sacrificed their lives to stand faithfully for the Lord Jesus. Reading these short stories aloud as a family will provoke your children to ask great questions and will promote deep discussions in your home. Another book, that surprisingly became a favorite of my daughter, Emily, was the little volume, *Final Words of the Dead and Dying*. When she first showed this book to me, I was concerned that it might be a little dark for my young daughter.

However, as she and I worked our way through this book, I saw the great spiritual growth it was promoting in her young life. This book contains the final words of both Christians and unbelievers. Seeing the vast difference in how these people faced their final moments was a defining time in my child's life. She was forced to consider how she would face death and to determine, would she die praising the Lord or cursing her circumstances? Obviously, a book like this would not be appropriate for all children, but the more we know our children and their heart conditions, the more accurately we will be able to help them to make good literary choices.

Please allow me to issue a word of caution concerning biographies that are more recently published. Especially in the arena of sports biographies, I would encourage you to pre-read any books that you allow your children to choose. Too often, today's sports "heroes" are esteemed simply because of their athletic ability or outrageous personalities. Whether or not these sports figures are people of high character seems unimportant to the average fan. Because of this trend, many of the newest biographies are peppered with foul language, immoral actions, and questionable ethics. Just because a baseball player throws a pitch at 99mph doesn't mean that his personal life will be any type of example for our children to follow. Having said that, there are still many sports personalities today with excellent testimonies and strong morals and beliefs. In particular, look for biographies of such athletes as: MaryLou Retton, Dave Draveky, Tony Dungy, and Curt Warner, and most recently, Tim Tebow.

Whatever the interests of your children, there are biographies to fill the need. Politics, inventions, exploration, homemaking, child-raising, you name it and I am sure you can find a biography to deepen your child's interest and understanding of the subject.

For moms, I have found the autobiographical books of Elizabeth Elliot to be inspirational and life changing. As well, the biographical *First We Have Coffee*, by Margaret Jensen, and the autobiographical *High Call, High Privilege*, by Gail MacDonald, were a great help to me as I was striving to grow and develop in my role as Pastor's wife. Reading biographies has helped me to continue to mature in the many areas of responsibility that I must fill. During the times that I have felt isolated, or when circumstances didn't permit me to attend a ladies bible study, biographies of strong Christian women served as a lifeline to provide fellowship, challenge, encouragement, and edification in my life.

Now, let's consider some biographies and works of historical fiction that you can incorporate into your home. Again, I am not advocating the use of historical romance novels and if I could, I would hold up a GIANT red flag at this point and say, "Stop, don't do it!" These books build a strong appetite for even more romance-centered books, and soon you will find your daughters living in a dream world of unrealistic young men who never make mistakes, always act lovingly, and choose them, over any other priority they might encounter. What a disappointment real life becomes when this unrealistic expectation is your measuring stick! As with other freedoms we allow in our children's lives, taking away these books after we have allowed or encouraged the reading of them, will cause strife and bitterness that is unprofitable and counter-productive in our homes. Proverbs 27:12 states, "A prudent man sees evil and hides himself, the naïve proceed and pay the penalty." This proverb is true in all areas of our parenting, but especially in our choices of the literature we do or do not allow our children to read. Romance novels, whether they are sold as historical fiction or not, build appetites for relationships and freedoms that our children should not have to face when they are young. Don't rush your children to desire these "grown-up" privileges. Allow them to be children and encourage them to use this short-lived time of their lives building life-long character, rather than premature romantic ideas!

One of the greatest series of biographical literature every written is the Landmark Book Series. Covering topics from George Washington, to the colonists, to the Revolutionary War, these books are well written and engrossing for both younger and more mature readers. Although the original Landmark books are out of print, you will easily find many reprints as the demand for these books amongst homeschoolers grows. If you find older copies at book sales or antique shops, they are well worth the money spent to purchase them.

A publisher of good historical fiction is Bob Jones Press. Their choice of topics and commitment to excellence has made these books favorites with all of my children. You can request a catalog online by searching the Bob Jones University website.

Biographical books for younger readers by Ingrid and Edgar Parin d'Aulaire are brimming with interesting and engaging historical facts and tidbits. As well, your children will find many historical friends in the books by Alice Dalgliesh. Both of these authors communicate in a warm and friendly style. I would use these books, while my children were very young, as read aloud books, and then, transition the same books into a read alone choice when the children were able to read on their own. Because the books are so enjoyable, the children didn't tire of reading to themselves the books that they had already enjoyed as family books, read aloud together.

For young adults, there are two different series of historical fiction books that have been especially appreciated by my sons. Although these books have also been read and enjoyed by my daughters, the manliness of the characters in the stories has been a real hook to capture the interest of my boys. The first series of books are the wide-ranging books by G.A. Henty. These exciting books draw children into the actual events of a time period, while introducing one fictional character. This character finds that he is thrust into the history and therefore, he must interact and make decisions about the events he sees unfolding. I appreciate that Henty does not make the moral decision-making process too easy for his young protagonists, but instead forces them to grapple with the implications and consequences of their decisions. Like the Landmark books, G.A. Henty books dropped out of publication for many years, but now have begun to be reprinted. Many older bookstores and antique shops yield a rich crop of the original Hentys.

When my son, Peter, was 12 years old, he could not get enough of G.A. Henty. At that time, it was difficult to find the older copies and new copies were just beginning to find their way to the bookshelves. What a blessing to receive a call from an older gentleman who had heard of Peter's love for the series. This man had written his Doctoral thesis on the works of G.A. Henty and had a true love and appreciation for the quality of the literature. Because he knew that his own grown children did not share his love for the Henty books, this generous man gave Peter his entire collection of first edition Henty's. Peter was overwhelmed and so grateful. This collection of books has become one of his most prized possessions and he has read all of the books over and over again. If you find that your child really loves a certain series of books, I would encourage you to get the word out. You never know what is stashed away in someone's garage or basement storage area that they would be thrilled to share with someone who would truly appreciate the gift!

Along with the G.A. Henty books, we have also enjoyed the books of historical fiction written by George Ballantine. These books follow the same general format as the books written by G.A. Henty, with a strong and character-driven fictional character placed into the real-life history of the stories. Ballantine, an outspoken Christian, wrote from a decidedly Christian perspective. Although Henty's books are from a very recognizable Christian worldview, you will recognize an even stronger emphasis on faith in the books by George Ballantine. The language and vocabulary that you will encounter in a Ballantine book is slightly more difficult than that which is found in the Henty series, so you might want to begin your children with Henty, and then progress to the Ballantine series. Again, reprints of the Ballantine books are becoming more readily available, but the older editions are an exciting find.

In pursuit of these out-of-print books, we have enjoyed many afternoons with our older children, scouring used bookstore shelves to look for first and second edition copies. Our children approach this time as a treasure hunt with exclamations of joy when a rarely seen book is procured. Perhaps not the usual "family-time" outing, but in our family of book lovers, time well spent!

As you search for great biographies for your children to read, don't overlook the great biographical works of literature about our Founding Fathers. Not only will your children be learning about the lives and heroic deeds of great men who were willing to sacrifice to begin this great country; they will also be reading first-hand about the desires of our forefathers in starting a New World, namely America. Through these biographies, your children will get a clearer picture of the intent of the Declaration of Independence and Constitution, than they would ever receive by simply reading about these documents in a history textbook. How much better to understand the principles on which our country was founded as explained by the men who put those principles in place, rather than simply reading someone's opinion about the founders original intentions. Biographies bring history to life, so utilize this resource at every opportunity.

Unlike the simply written diary/biographies published by Scholastic books, diaries of our Founding Fathers are rich resources to learn more about the hardships involved in starting this country. Through diaries of men like: Benjamin Franklin, George Washington, and William Bradford, your children will learn what it meant, on a personal level, for these men to participate in the rebellion against England and the hard work of planting a new country. They will interact with these men's great thoughts and petty grievances. Long ago figures will come alive as your children empathize, disagree with, and root for these very real men.

Searching for great biographical literature is like the treasure hunt of looking for well-preserved old books. Sometimes the job is tedious and exhausting, while at other times you will find a biography of a little known person who has an important lesson to teach you and your children. Enjoy the hunt! A love for great biographical literature is the treasure you will unearth in the process.

DANGER! DANGER!

Even the good things that enter our lives have the potential to cause harm at some level. The Internet has provided access to information in a way that our own parents could never have imagined. However, with this vast array of information, has come the capacity to download just as vast an array of morally violating and potentially dangerous materials. Food, while delicious, enjoyable and necessary to supply the energy we need to fulfill our daily duties, when consumed in an unhealthy or in an overly abundant way, can cause ill health and long-term weight problems.

The same inherent dangers can be found in exercise, rest, relationships, etc. Literature is no exception. Although literature, and especially great literature, has an abundance of positive attributes, even within this medium dangers are lurking.

There are probably many dangers you could think of when considering the use of literature in your home. I would like to focus on three areas of danger in particular. The first area concerns us, as parents, and our attitudes toward reading in general. The second danger involves books that insult our children's inherent intelligence, and the third danger is an overuse of any particular type of literature.

Let's begin with danger number one, parental attitudes toward reading and reading choices. I don't believe that there is a responsible parent alive that doesn't want their child to be an avid reader of great literature. Having said that, however, as parents we can help or hinder the process. As previously stated, we help the process by providing great literature, by reading aloud, by modeling reading ourselves, and by challenging our children to digest more and more difficult books. How then, do we become parents that hinder, rather than help our children in their journey toward a love of literature?

Too often, as parents, we settle for our children reading whatever they want, just as long as they are reading. I have been dismayed to hear parents excitedly talk about the large quantity of really trashy books that their children are reading. These parents will sigh in relief, "At least they're reading SOMETHING!" What??? Do we really believe that quantity is more important than quality? Although I don't believe that any of us would admit to encouraging such a belief, our actions can communicate that very concept to our children. Parents, we are the guardians of our children's hearts until they are old enough to make good and Godly decisions on their own. Do not allow the prevailing book choices of a group of young children to decide what your child is reading. You be in charge!

Honestly, this attitude is the same as a parent watching their twelve-year old child down a cold can of beer and saying, "Well, at least they are hydrated!" A ridiculous notion, but no more ridiculous than settling for low-quality and morally questionable reading material, just to get your child reading. This is no time to turn a blind eye and relax Godly standards.

The Word of God states clearly in I Corinthians 10:23, "All things are lawful, but not all things are profitable. All things are lawful, but not all things edify." Just because our children CAN read certain books is not an indication that they SHOULD read those books. Morally corrupt characters and situations, enjoyed as reading material from a young age, will plant seeds of rebellion in your child and disintegration in your home. Practice discernment and do not be afraid to tell your child NO. Make sure that instead, you have an abundant supply of positive and morally uplifting literature available and easily accessible.

This problem of children reading an abundance of books, without the books representing any real value, and in fact, representing potential harm, is nothing new. Consider carefully this excerpt from the book, *Eight Cousins*, written by Louisa May Alcott and published in 1874. Although the excerpt is a bit long, please read it through and consider whether or not the problem encountered in that time is any different than the dilemma we face today in assisting our children to make wise reading choices.

""I wish Rose would drive a bargain with Will and Geordie also, for I think these books are as bad for the small boys as cigars for the large ones," said Mrs. Jessie, sitting down on the sofa between the readers, who politely curled up their legs to make room for her.

"I thought they were all the fashion," answered Dr. Alec, settling in the big chair with Rose.

"So is smoking, but it is harmful. The writers of these popular stories intend to do good, I have no doubt, but it seems to me they fail because their motto is, 'Be smart, and you will be rich,' instead of 'Be honest, and you will be happy.' I do not judge hastily, Alec, for I have read a dozen, at least, of these stories, and, with much that is attractive to boys, I find a great deal to condemn in them, and other parents say the same when I ask them."
"Now, Mum, that's too bad! I like 'em tip-top. This one is a regular screamer," cried Will.

"They're bully books, and I'd like to know where's the harm," added Geordie.

"You have just shown us one of the chief evils, and that is slang," answered their mother quickly. "Must have it, ma'am. If these chaps talked all right, there'd be no fun in 'em," protested Will.

"A boot-black mustn't use good grammar, and a newsboy must swear a little, or he wouldn't be natural," explained Geordie, both boys ready to fight gallantly for their favourites.

"But my sons are neither boot-blacks nor newsboys, and I object to hearing them use such words as 'screamer,' 'bully,' and 'buster.' In fact, I fail to see the advantage of writing books about such people unless it is done in a very different way. I cannot think they will help to refine the ragamuffins if they read them, and I'm sure they can do no good to the better class of boys, who through these books are introduced to police courts, counterfeiters' dens, gambling houses, drinking saloons, and all sorts of low life."

"Some of them are about first-rate boys, mother; and they go to sea and study, and sail round the world, having great larks all the way."

"I have read about them, Geordie, and though they are better than the others, I am not satisfied with these optical delusions, as I call them. Now, I put it to you, boys, is it natural for lads from fifteen to eighteen to command ships, defeat pirates, outwit smugglers, and so cover themselves with glory, that Admiral Farragut invites them to dinner, saying, 'Noble boy, you are an honour to your country!' Or, if the hero is in the army, he has hair-breadth escapes and adventures enough in one small volume to turn his hair white, and in the end he goes to Washington at the express desire of the President or Commander-in-chief to be promoted to no end of stars and bars. Even if the hero is merely an honest boy trying to get his living, he is not permitted to do so in a natural way, by hard work and years of patient effort, but is suddenly adopted by a millionaire whose pocket-book he has returned; or a rich uncle appears from sea just in the nick of time; or the remarkable boy earns a few dollars, speculates in pea-nuts or neckties, and grows rich so rapidly that Sinbad in the diamond valley is a pauper compared to him. Isn't it so, boys?"

"Well, the fellows in these books are mighty lucky, and very smart, I must say," answered Will, surveying an illustration on the open page before him, where a small but virtuous youth is upsetting a tipsy giant in a bar-room, and under it the elegant inscription, "Dick Dauntless punches the head of Sam Soaker."

"It gives boys such wrong ideas of life and business; shows them so much evil and vulgarity that they need not know about, and makes the one success worth having a fortune, a lord's daughter, or some worldly honour, often not worth the time it takes to win. It does seem to me that some one might write stories that should be lively, natural and helpful tales in which the English should be good, the morals pure, and the characters such as we can love in spite of the faults that all may have. I can't bear to see such crowds of eager little fellows at the libraries reading such trash; weak, when it is not wicked, and totally unfit to feed the hungry minds that feast on it for want of something better. There! my lecture is done; now I should like to hear what you gentlemen have to say," and Aunt Jessie subsided with a pretty flush on the face that was full of motherly anxiety for her boys.

"Tom Brown just suits mother, and me too, so I wish Mr. Hughes would write another story as good," said Archie.

"You don't find things of this sort in Tom Brown; yet these books are all in the Sunday-school libraries" and Mrs. Jessie read the following paragraph from the book she had taken from Will's hand,

"'In this place we saw a tooth of John the Baptist. Ben said he could see locust and wild honey sticking to it. I couldn't. Perhaps John used a piece of the true cross for a tooth-pick.'"

"A larky sort of a boy says that, Mum, and we skip the parts where they describe what they saw in the different countries," cried Will.

"And those descriptions, taken mostly from guidebooks, I fancy, are the only parts of any real worth. The scrapes of the bad boys make up the rest of the story, and it is for those you read these books, I think," answered his mother, stroking back the hair off the honest little face that looked rather abashed at this true statement of the case. "Anyway, mother, the ship part is useful, for we learn how to sail her, and by and by that will all come handy when we go to sea," put in Geordie. "Indeed, then you can explain this manoeuvre to me, of course," and Mrs. Jessie read from another page the following nautical paragraph,

"The wind is south-south-west, and we can have her up four points closer to the wind, and still be six points off the wind. As she luffs up we shall man the fore and main sheets, slack on the weather, and haul on the lee braces."

"I guess I could, if I wasn't afraid of uncle. He knows so much more than I do, he'd laugh," began Geordie, evidently puzzled by the question.

"Ho, you know you can't, so why make believe? We don't understand half of the sea lingo, Mum, and I dare say it's all wrong," cried Will, suddenly going over to the enemy, to Geordie's great disgust. "I do wish the boys wouldn't talk to me as if I was a ship," said Rose, bringing forward a private grievance. "Coming home from church this morning, the wind blew me about, and Will called out, right in the street, 'Brail up the foresail, and take in the flying-jib, that will ease her.'"

The boys shouted at the plaintive tone in which Rose repeated the words that offended her, and Will vainly endeavoured to explain that he only meant to tell her to wrap her cloak closer, and tie a veil over the tempest-tossed feathers in her hat. "To tell the truth, if the boys must have slang, I can bear the 'sea lingo,' as Will calls it, better than the other. It afflicts me less to hear my sons talk about 'brailing up the foresail' than doing as they 'darn please,' and 'cut your cable' is decidedly preferable to 'let her rip.' I once made a rule that I would have no slang in the house. I give it up now, for I cannot keep it; but I will not have rubbishy books; so, Archie, please send these two after your cigars." Mrs. Jessie held both the small boys fast with an arm round each neck, and when she took this base advantage of them they could only squirm with dismay. "Yes, right behind the back log," she continued, energetically. "There, my hearties (you like sea slang, so I'll give you a bit) now, I want you to promise not to read any more stuff for a month, and I'll agree to supply you with wholesome fare."

"Oh, mother, not a single one?" cried Will.

"Couldn't we just finish those?" pleaded Geordie. "The boys threw away half-smoked cigars; and your books must go after them. Surely you would not be outdone by the 'old fellows,' as you call them, or be less obedient to little Mum than they were to Rose."

"Course not! Come on, Geordie," and Will took the vow like a hero. His brother sighed and obeyed, but privately resolved to finish his story the minute the month was over."

Now, as then, vigilance was in order to protect the moral character of our young people. Parents... The responsibility is ours! Let's not be lax in promoting the positive, prohibiting the negative, and teaching the difference between the two!

The second area of danger that I see in children's literature is the enormous amount of books written that insult our children's intelligence and often produce the exact opposite of what we are hoping to teach our children. Especially in the "Christian" book realm, these books seem to be the easy, go-to, shortcut books to teach character lessons. I am talking about the books that announce the lesson that they are intended to teach, then use the announced quality over and over in the text. For example: books such as *Chief So-and-So Learns To Tell the Truth,* or *Sally's Book of Sharing.* (Obviously, I made up the titles to protect the guilty!)

Please, give your children more credit than this! In essence, these books are nothing more than a multi-paged lecture on the needed character quality. As adults, we would be repulsed by anyone handing us a book to read, or reading a book aloud to us, regarding some lack they saw in our character development. I believe that our children are just as repulsed by these inferior offerings. These books are about as effective as a wife laying a "How To Be a Great Husband" book on the coffee table for their husband to happen upon. Don't Do It! There is no need to settle for these types of books and there is a much better alternative.

These books are not works of great literature. Too often, the characters in the book begin the story by making terrible character choices. Predictably, in a few short pages they have come to their senses and promise never to make such a mistake again. Wouldn't it be better to introduce our children to characters who choose to make the right choice in the first-place? Or, characters whom face the consequences of their bad decisions and learn life-long lessons, rather than making quick and momentary decisions to avoid the lesson and simply bring an end to the problem at hand?

I am convinced that our children, even the youngest children, have an amazing capacity to recognize and learn character lessons from great literature, without us ever needing to intentionally point out the intended lesson. How much better for our children to internalize these lessons independently, without feeling coerced to "see the lesson, learn the lesson, live the lesson." Obviously, our children need extensive times of our verbal instruction. They need moms and dads that are willing to spend massive quantities of time teaching them important lessons of character and moral growth. We should and must take that time. What they don't need is a book to cram the lesson down their throat. Great books with great characters will gently lead them to the right conclusions without insulting their intelligence or assuming they just can't recognize the lesson on their own.

Finally, there is a great danger in allowing too many books of any certain type. Fantasy books, in moderation, can be an acceptable form of reading. However, fantasy books read to the exclusion of all other types will build appetites for the unreal and a lopsided child. In the same way, princess books, while not the greatest literature, can be an allowable genre. However, please don't allow your girls to only read this form of literature. Believe me, I have four daughters and the days that any of them are in "Princess" mode are the hardest days in our home. I, the scullery maid, invariably have to drag them back to reality!

The adults that we enjoy the most are the adults with a well-rounded personality. We like to spend time with people whom can converse intelligently on a variety of subjects, regardless of their own special areas of interest. Johnny-One-Notes are tolerable to spend time with to a point, but they soon lose their audience. Helping our children to become well-rounded adults with a wide variety of interests is one of our responsibilities as caring parents. Mixing up the genre they read will become a positive step in the right direction.

Often, my children would become engrossed in a certain series of books, breathlessly awaiting the newest installment. There is nothing wrong with such anticipation. However, if I noticed that the next series of books they chose looked almost identical to the last series in plot, storyline, and character type, I made it a point to redirect their interest. Although I sometimes had to deal with disappointment and a bit of grumbling, invariably, they found the new books I introduced them to equally interesting and soon they were off on a new literary adventure.

Even allowable books, when chosen to the exclusion of all others, can become an appetite that we need to help our children to suppress. There is a difference between enjoyment of a certain type of literature and addiction to that literature. You will need to help your children learn to discern the difference. Even too much allegorical literature can lead to an imbalance in your child's development. Help them to choose a wide variety of well written, thought provoking, great literature. Although they may dislike the limitations you place on them at this point, they will be thankful for their wide-ranging portfolio of literary interests in the future.

Don't let the dangerous side of literature frighten you! Spend the time and effort necessary to research and provide great literature for your children. Help your children choose literature that is brimming with positive life lessons and applications; literature that assumes your child is intelligent and insightful. Finally, search out literature that captivates your child's heart without ensnaring or addicting them in an unhealthy way.

"There is a difference between enjoyment of a certain type of literature and addiction to that literature. You will need to help your children learn to discern the difference."

www.characterhealth.com

SOME NOT-SO-GREAT LITERATURE (BUT, REALLY FUN BOOKS)

This chapter is my opportunity to share with you some books that will never share accolades with the great books of classic literature. These books will never be studied for years in our high school classrooms. These books don't have moving language or heart wrenching drama. HOWEVER, these books are just plain fun and many teach important lessons in a humorous and definitely non-threatening way!

There have been numerous times in our home that my children have already been taught an important character lesson through verbal instruction and even using great literature to back up the concept. Nevertheless, it becomes obvious to me that the lesson needs some fine-tuning, some reminding, some tweaking and refining. I could try to re-teach these lessons with a wordy lecture, (never works by the way). I could have my children write me a two-paged paper explaining the missing character quality, (Boy oh boy, wouldn't they love that!) I could explode and berate them for their lack of consistency, (Really doesn't work!) Or, I could pull out some of our humorous books, that incidentally teach some great character, too.

In this category, two particular series come to mind. The first is the *Mrs. Piggle-Wiggle* Series. Granted, these books do contain some magic, of the upside down house type, but the lessons that my children learned through Mrs. Piggle-Wiggle's creative solutions to everyday problems was well worth the time spent explaining the magic. These books, by Betty MacDonald, deal with such daily character issues as: grumbling, dawdling, coveting, quarreling, laziness, embellishment, and the list goes on and on. As we read the books aloud, laughing together at the outrageous behavior of the children in Mrs. Piggle-Wiggle's town, my children could easily recognize themselves. I never had to say, "Gosh, that reminds me of someone I know," the children would diagnose their own problem areas and together we would chuckle over Mrs. Piggle-Wiggle's cures. Even today, the children will threaten to use one of her cures on each other, or sometimes, even on their Father and me.

The second series of books we enjoyed was the *George and Martha* books by James Marshall. The lovable hippopotamus' in this series teach character lessons in a humorous and absolutely endearing manner. Watching Martha console George when he lost his tooth (His favorite one) was a great life lesson in compassion and empathy. Likewise, when Martha caught George watching her bathe, through peals of laughter my children easily recognized the lessons regarding privacy. George and Martha deal with offended feelings, not telling the whole truth, ridicule, and more. Sometimes, after the children are in bed, my husband and I still sit together on the couch laughing at the silly stories and awesome illustrations in George and Martha.

Looking for a fun way to teach your children about the peculiarities of the English language? The Amelia Bedelia books by Herman Parish will teach your children to use our language properly, even as they guffaw at Amelia Bedelia's outrageous mistakes. Although Amelia Bedelia is a grown-up, her childlike approach to life will ingratiate this character to your children. Our family incorporates many "Amelia Bedeliaisms" into our daily activities and conversation!

Obviously, they are not great works of literature; nonetheless the early Nancy Drew and Hardy Boys books introduce teenaged characters with some great character qualities. Nancy, Frank, and Joe are always polite, neatly dressed, gracious, and others oriented. Honestly, sometimes I feel like telling my children, "Why can't you be more like Nancy?" I am *not* including the newer books of these series in my recommendation. Sadly, the newer versions are as much romance novels as they are mystery stories. The older books however, will encourage your children to be inventors, initiators, and pro-active problem solvers. The characters in these books are respectful to their parents and eager to seek help and counsel from adults. I would love for my children to be characterized in this same way. As well, the characters in both series surround themselves with friends that adhere to the same high caliber of moral character.

The Henry and Mudge series of books, authored by Cynthia Rylant, are a nice way to encourage your new readers to begin independent reading.

The books don't necessarily try to teach any deep lessons, but instead are simple stories of the everyday life of Henry and his beloved dog Mudge. Children, reading about Henry's adventures, will begin to see their daily lives as a time of adventure as well. Not at all a bad way to look at life!

All of my children have gone through a *Nate the Great* phase. These detective books, written by Marjorie Weinman Sharmat and Marc Simont, will inspire your children to turn every lost sock and misplaced schoolbook into the next great mystery to be solved. My two youngest boys are enjoying the books at this point and almost every day they inquire if I am missing anything. Since they want to charge me for their services, I am skeptical when they point out articles they believe are "misplaced." We have always had great fun watching the children re-enacting their favorite Nate the Great stories.

If you are looking for some just silly, laugh aloud books with memorable characters, turn to the *Hank the Cowdog* books by John R. Erickson. As the Head of Ranch Security, Hank finds himself in ridiculous situation after ridiculous situation. I could always tell when my son was reading about Hank during his rest hour because of the uncontrollable giggles coming from his room. Hank has quite a following and you can even purchase Hank t-shirts and games.

I'm not encouraging you to feed your children a steady diet of these just-for-fun books, but don't take life so seriously that you never stop to read something just for the fun of it. No, they may not be learning any deep life lessons, but your children will be learning what it means to just relax and have fun with the friends they make in these humorous books.

Finally, and in a spirit of total self-promotion, I really love the new series of books written by my husband Steve and myself! Using our children's total and continual lack of proper noun usage as a jumping off point, we developed the *King of Thing and the Kingdom of Thingdom* books. Imagine a land where no one and nothing has a name; *that's* the Kingdom of Thingdom. Pick up Book One to meet the King, his wife Katherine, his twin sons This and That, and his teenage daughter, Whatever. Join them as they travel through the Kingdom greeting the Hey-You's and visiting the red-building-where-the mooey-milky-thing lives with Farmer What's-His-Name. Subsequent titles in the series include: *The King of Thing and the Epic Pun War*, *The King of Thing and the Terror of Texting*, *The King of Thing and the California Cousin*, and *The King of Thing and the Maine Vacation*.

Reading is fun! Pick up some fun books today and have a hilarious family night together, on the couch, sharing the adventures of some not-so-great-literature, but really fun books!

There is no better time than today! Get your families started on the journey of building a lifelong affection for great books, for biographies and historical fiction, and for some just-for fun books, simply intended to brighten your day. Whatever type of literature you are looking for... there's a book that's just right for you and your family. Enjoy the adventure!

Megan Ann

> *"Reading is fun! Pick up some fun books today and have a hilarious family night together, on the couch, sharing the adventures of some not-so-great-literature, but really fun books!"*

www.characterhealth.com

LITERATURE LIST: BOOKS WE LOVE TO READ

Obviously, reading and books are an important part of our day. Below, you'll find some of the books that we have loved; books that we've returned to over and over. I hesitate to put ages with books, since reading ability and age are so variable. Although there are some wonderful books that have been written in recent years, in general, I find that the older books do a more thorough job of clearly presenting good and evil.

As well, while there are certainly exceptions to this rule, older books tend to have less questionable material. With newer selections, I try to take time to peruse the book myself, before passing it off to my children.

I have added a space for you to fill in when you have read a book to your children. Too often I would think back on the books we had read and realize that 4 of our children hadn't even been born yet! Hopefully this will help to keep that from happening to you.

Reading Resources

Read Aloud:

- Good Night Moon — Margaret Wise Brown
  Date: _____

- The Runaway Bunny — Margaret Wise Brown
  Date: _____

- The Little Fur Family — Margaret Wise Brown
  Date: _____

- The Little Fisherman — Margaret Wise Brown
  Date: _____

- Time of Wonder — Robert McCloskey
  Date: _____

- One Morning in Maine — Robert McCloskey
  Date: _____

- Make Way For Ducklings — Robert McCloskey
  Date: _____

- Blueberries For Sal — Robert McCloskey
  Date: _____

- The Steadfast Tin Soldier —
  Hans Christian Anderson
  Date: _____

- The Very Busy Spider — Eric Carle
  Date: _____

- The Very Clumsy Click Beetle — Eric Carle
  Date: _____

- The Very Hungry Caterpillar — Eric Carle
  Date: _____

- The Very Lonely Firefly — Eric Carle
  Date: _____

- The Very Quiet Cricket — Eric Carle
  Date: _____

- Mike Mulligan and His Steam Shovel
  — Virginia Lee Burton
  Date: _____

- Katy and the Big Snow — Virginia Lee Burton
  Date: _____

- The Little Engine That Could — Watty Piper
  Date: _____

- The Relatives Came — Cynthia Rylant
  Date: _____

- Caps For Sale — Esphyr Slobodkina
  Date: _____

- The Story About Ping — Marjorie Flack
  Date: _____

Early Readers:

- Tacky The Penguin — Helen Lester
  Date: _____

- Little Black a Pony — Walter Farley
  Date: _____

- A Fly Went By — Mike McClintock
  Date: _____

- "B" Is For Betsy — Carolyn Haywood
  Date: _____

- Betsy and Billy — Carolyn Haywood
  Date: _____

- Back To School With Betsy — Carolyn Haywood
  Date: _____

- Betsy and the Boys — Carolyn Haywood
  Date: _____

- Betsy's Little Star — Carolyn Haywood
  Date: _____

- Betsy and the Circus — Carolyn Haywood
  Date: _____

- Betsy's Busy Summer — Carolyn Haywood
  Date: _____

- Betsy's Winterhouse — Carolyn Haywood
  Date: _____

- Snowbound With Betsy — Carolyn Haywood
  Date: _____

- Betsy and Mr. Kilpatrick — Carolyn Haywood
  Date: _____

- Pollyanna — Eleanor H. Porter
  Date: _____

- Betsy — Tacy — Maud Hart Lovelace
  Date: _____

- Betsy — Tacy and Tib — Maud Hart Lovelace
  Date: _____

- Betsy and Tacy Go Over the Big Hill
  — Maud Hart Lovelace
  Date: _____

- Betsy and Tacy Go Downtown
  — Maud Hart Lovelace
  Date: _____

- Heaven To Betsy — Maud Hart Lovelace
  Date: _____

- Betsy In Spite of Herself — Maud Hart Lovelace
  Date: _____

- Betsy Was a Junior — Maud Hart Lovelace
  Date: _____

- Betsy and Joe — Maud Hart Lovelace
  Date: _____

- Betsy and the Great World — Maud Hart Lovelace
  Date: _____

- Betsy's Wedding — Maud Hart Lovelace
  Date: _____

- Nancy Drew series
  — those copyrighted prior to 1980
  Date: _____

- The Hardy Boys series
  — copyrighted prior to 1959
  Date: _____

- The Bobbsey Twins series
  — copyrighted prior to 1979
  Date: _____

- The Boxcar Children series
  — Gertrude Chandler Warner
  Date: _____

- All of a Kind Family — Sydney Taylor
  Date: _____

- All of a Kind Family Downtown — Sydney Taylor
  Date: _____

- More All of a Kind Family — Sydney Taylor
  Date: _____

- All of a Kind Family Uptown — Sydney Taylor
  Date: _____

- Ella of All of a Kind Family — Sydney Taylor
  Date: _____

- Henry and Mudge — Cynthia Rylant
  Date: _____

- Nate the Great — Marjorie Weinman
  Date: _____

- Hank the Cowdog — John R. Erikson
  Date: _____

- Golly Sisters series — Betsy Byars
  Date: _____

- The King of Thing — Steve and Megan Scheibner
  Date: _____

- Frog and Toad series — Arnold Lobel
  Date: _____

- Danger at the Breaker — Catherine Welch
  Date: _____

- Keep the Lights Burning, Abbie
  — Peter and Connie Roop
  Date: _____

- The Courage of Sarah Noble — Alice Dalgliesh
  Date: _____

- Sarah Plain and Tall — Patricia MacLachlan
  Date: _____

- George and Martha — James Marshall
  Date: _____

- Amelia Bedelia — Herman Parish
  Date: _____

- Baby — Patricia MacLachlan
  Date: _____

- The Bears on Hemlock Mountain — Alice Dalgliesh
  Date: _____

- Mrs. Piggle — Wiggle — Betty MacDonald
  Date: _____

- Baby Island — Carol Ryrie Brink
  Date: _____

- Mice of the Nine Lives — Tim Davis
  Date: _____

- Mice of the Herring Bone — Tim Davis
  Date: _____

- Mice of the Seven Seas — Tim Davis
  Date: _____

- Mice of the Westing Wind — Tim Davis
  Date: _____

- Captive Treasure — Milly Howard
  Date: _____

- The Bridge — Jeri Massi
  Date: _____

- Crown and Jewel — Jeri Massi
  Date: _____

- The Two Collars — Jeri Massi
  Date: _____

- Understood Betsy — Dorothy Canfield Fisher
  Date: _____

- With Daring Faith — Rebecca Davis
  Date: _____

- The Year of Jubilo — Ruth Sawyer
  Date: _____

- Thee, Hannah — Marguerite de Angeli
  Date: _____

- Henner's Lydia — Marguerite de Angeli
  Date: _____

- Copper — Toed Boots — Marguerite de Angeli
  Date: _____

- Petite Suzanne — Marguerite de Angeli
  Date: _____

- Tom Swift series — copyrighted prior to 1971
  Date: _____

- Little House In the Big Woods
  — Laura Ingalls Wilder
  Date: _____

- Farmer Boy — Laura Ingalls Wilder
  Date: _____

- Little House on the Prairie — Laura Ingalls Wilder
  Date: _____

- On the Banks of Plum Creek
  — Laura Ingalls Wilder
  Date: _____

- By the Shores of Silver Lake — Laura Ingalls Wilder
  Date: _____

- The Long Winter — Laura Ingalls Wilder
  Date: _____

- Little Town on the Prairie — Laura Ingalls Wilder *Date:* _____

- These Happy Golden Years — Laura Ingalls Wilder
  Date: _____

- Black Beauty — Anna Sewall
  Date: _____

- The Black Stallion — Walter Farley
  Date: _____

- The Black Stallion Returns — Walter Farley
  Date: _____

- Misty of Chincoteague — Marguerite Henry
  Date: _____

- Justin Morgan Had a Horse — Marguerite Henry

  Date: _____

- King of the Wind — Marguerite Henry

  Date: _____

- Sea Star, Orphan of Chincoteague
  — Marguerite Henry

  Date: _____

- Born to Trot — Marguerite Henry

  Date: _____

- Brighty of the Grand Canyon — Marguerite
  Henry *Date:* _____

- Stormy, Misty's Foal — Marguerite Henry

  Date: _____

- White Stallion of Lipizza — Marguerite Henry

  Date: _____

- Misty's Twilight — Marguerite Henry

  Date: _____

- The Lion, the Witch, and the Wardrobe
  — C.S. Lewis
  Date: _____

- Prince Caspian — C.S. Lewis
  Date: _____

- The Voyage of the Dawn Treader — C.S. Lewis
  Date: _____

- The Silver Chair — C.S. Lewis
  Date: _____

- The Horse and His Boy — C.S. Lewis
  Date: _____

- The Magician's Nephew — C.S. Lewis
  Date: _____

- The Last Battle — C.S. Lewis
  Date: _____

- Farmer Giles of Ham — J.R.R. Tolkien
  Date: _____

Older Readers:

*   The Wind in the Willows — Kenneth Grahame
    Date: _____

*   Lost on a Mountain In Maine — Donn Fendler
    Date: _____

*   Island of the Blue Dolphins — Scott O'Dell
    Date: _____

*   Elsie Dinsmore series — Martha Finley
    Date: _____

*   Johnny Tremain — Esther Forbes
    Date: _____

*   Dust of the Earth — Donna Hess
    Date: _____

*   The Lost Prince — Frances Hodgson Burnett
    Date: _____

*   Robinson Crusoe — Daniel Defoe
    Date: _____

- Apples To Oregon
  — Deborah Hopkinson and Mary Carpenter
  Date: _____

- A Little Princess — Frances Hodgson Burnett
  Date: _____

- Hans Brinker and the Silver Skates
  — Mary Maples Dodge
  Date: _____

- Calico Bush — Rachel Field
  Date: _____

- Carry On Mr. Bowditch — Jean Lee Latham
  Date: _____

- Eight Cousins — Louisa May Alcott
  Date: _____

- Rose In Bloom — Louisa May Alcott
  Date: _____

- Little Women — Louisa May Alcott
  Date: _____

- Little Men — Louisa May Alcott
  Date: _____

- Under the Lilacs — Louisa May Alcott
  Date: _____

- An Old Fashioned Girl — Louisa May Alcott
  Date: _____

- The Hobbit — J.R.R. Tolkien
  Date: _____

- The Fellowship of the Ring — J.R.R. Tolkien
  Date: _____

- The Two Towers — J.R.R. Tolkien
  Date: _____

- The Return of the King — J.R.R. Tolkien
  Date: _____

- Treasures of the Snow — Patricia St. John
  Date: _____

- Star of Light — Patricia St. John
  Date: _____

- The Tanglewoods' Secret — Patricia St. John
  Date: _____

- Rainbow Garden — Patricia St. John
  Date: _____

- Anne of Green Gables
  — Lucy Maude Montgomery
  Date: _____

- Anne of the Island — Lucy Maude Montgomery
  Date: _____

- Anne of Avonlea — Lucy Maude Montgomery
  Date: _____

- Anne's House of Dreams
  — Lucy Maude Montgomery
  Date: _____

- Rainbow Valley — Lucy Maude Montgomery
  Date: _____

- Roll of Thunder Hear My Cry
  — Mildred D. Taylor
  Date: _____

- Big Red — Jim Kjelgaard
  Date: _____

- Snow Dog — Jim Kjelgaard
  Date: _____

- Irish Red, Son of Big Red — Jim Kjelgaard
  Date: _____

- Outlaw Red, Son of Big Red — Jim Kjelgaard
  Date: _____

- Desert Dog — Jim Kjelgaard
  Date: _____

- Tom Sawyer — Mark Twain
  Date: _____

- A Girl of the Limberlost — Gene Stratton Porter
  Date: _____

- Freckles — Gene Stratton Porter
  Date: _____

- The Harvester — Gene Stratton Porter
  Date: _____

- Not My Will — Fancena H. Arnold
  Date: _____

- Stepping Heavenward — Elizabeth Prentiss
  Date: _____

- The Count of Monte Cristo — Alexandre Dumas
  Date: _____

- Ben Hur — Lew Wallace
  Date: _____

- Emma — Jane Austen
  Date: _____

- Drums — James Boyd
  Date: _____

- Treasure Island — Robert Louis Stevenson
  Date: _____

- A Tale of Two Cities — Charles Dickens
  Date: _____

- 20,000 Leagues Under the Sea — Jules Verne
  Date: _____

- The Mysterious Island — Jules Verne
  Date: _____

- Scottish Chiefs — Jane Porter
  Date: _____

- The Swiss Family Robinson — Johann Wyss
  Date: _____

- Robinson Crusoe — Daniel Defoe
  Date: _____

- Peter Pan — J.M. Barrie
  Date: _____

- The Kings Swift Rider – Mollie Hunter
  Date: _____

- The Black Arrow — Robert Louis Stevenson
  Date: _____

- Pilgrims Progress— John Bunyan
  Date: _____

- Last of the Mohicans
  — James Fenimore Cooper
  Date: _____

- The Adventures of Sherlock Holmes
  — Sir Arthur Conan Doyle
  Date: _____

- Les Miserable – Victor Hugo
  Date: _____

- The Hunchback of Notre Dame — Victor Hugo
  Date: _____

- Moby Dick — Herman Melville
  Date: _____

- Ivanhoe — Sir Walter Scott
  Date: _____

- The Strange Case of Dr. Jekyll and Mr. Hyde
  — Robert Louis Stevenson
  Date: _____

- Kidnapped — Robert Louis Stevenson
  Date: _____

- Around the World in 80 Days — Jules Verne
  Date: _____

- Lorna Dorne — R.D. Blackmore
  Date: _____

- Jane Eyre — Charlotte Bronte
  Date: _____

- The Scarlet Letter — Nathaniel Hawthorne
  Date: _____

- The Odyssey — Homer
  Date: _____

- The Illiad — Homer
  Date: _____

- The Jungle Book — Rudyard Kipling
  Date: _____

- Red Badge of Courage — Stephen Crane
  Date: _____

- A Christmas Carol — Charles Dickens
  Date: _____

- Great Expectations — Charles Dickens
  Date: _____

- Arabian Knights — unknown
  Date: _____

- Man In the Iron Mask — Alexander Dumas
  Date: _____

- Frankenstein — Mary Shelley
  Date: _____

- A Connecticut Yankee in King Arthur's Court
  — Mark Twain
  Date: _____

- Time Machine — H.G. Wells
  Date: _____

- War of the Worlds — H.G.Wells
  Date: _____

- The Three Musketeer — Alexander Dumas
  Date: _____

- The Prince and the Pauper — Mark Twain
  Date: _____

- Roverandom — J.R.R. Tolkien
  Date: _____

- The Silmarillion — J.R.R. Tolkien
  Date: _____

- The Biography of Stonewall Jackson
  — James Robertson
  Date: _____

- All G.A. Henty books
  Date: _____

- Books in the Landmark history series
  Date: _____

- Making Home Happy — L.D. Avery — Stuttle
  Date: _____

Books to Encourage Your Heart
And Inspire Your Imagination

* Homeschooling With a Meek and Quiet Spirit
  — Teri Maxwell
  Date: _____

* Desiring God — John Piper
  Date: _____

* Don't Waste Your Life — John Piper
  Date: _____

* The Mission of Motherhood — Sally Clarkson
  Date: _____

* The Ministry of Motherhood — Sally Clarkson
  Date: _____

* Educating the Wholehearted Child
  — Sally Clarkson
  Date: _____

- Seasons of a Mother's Heart — Sally Clarkson

  Date: _____

- Dancing With My Father — Sally Clarkson

  Date: _____

- The Mom Walk: Keeping
  in Step with God's Heart

  Date: _____

- For Motherhood — Sally Clarkson

  Date: _____

- My Heart's at Home — Jill Savage

  Date: _____

- Discipline, The Glad Surrender
  — Elizabeth Elliot

  Date: _____

- The Shaping of a Christian Family
  — Elizabeth Elliot

  Date: _____

- The Fulfilled Family — John MacArthur
  Date: _____

- The Successful Christian Homeschool Family
  — Raymond and Dorothy Moore
  Date: _____

- What Is a Family — Edith Schaeffer
  Date: _____

- The Most Important Place on Earth
  — Robert Wolgemuth
  Date: _____

- The Mentoring Mom — Jackie Kendall
  Date: _____

- First We Have Coffee — Margaret Jenson
  Date: _____

- Reaping the Harvest: The Bounty
  of Abundant Life Homeschooling
  — Diana Waring
  Date: _____

- Beyond Survival: A Guide to
  Abundant Life Homeschooling
  — Diana Waring
  Date: _____

- Things We Wish We'd Known
  — compiled by Diana Waring
  Date: _____

- Homeschooling: A Patchwork of Days
  — compiled by Nancy Lande
  Date: _____

- Homeschool Open House
  — compiled by Nancy Lande
  Date: _____

- Romancing Your Child's Heart — Monte Swan
  Date: _____

- Hearth and Home: Recipes For Life — Karey Swan
  Date: _____

- Secret Keeper, The Delicate Power of Modesty
  — Dannah Gresh
  Date: _____

- The Purity Principle — Randy Alcorn
  Date: _____

- Looking At Myself Before Loving Someone Else
  cJohn Coblentz
  Date: _____

RECIPE SECTION

LUNCH BARS

As I said in the introduction, lunches do not need to be complicated. Often, the leftovers and odds and ends in our refrigerators will make the best and most memorable lunches for our families. However, even leftovers can be made more appetizing by a unique or inviting presentation. I am not talking about time-consuming meal preparation, but simply taking what you will already be serving and creatively turning the food into a "food bar." My children love when food is served in this manner and I am sure that your children will feel the same.

One of the greatest assets of the food bar system is the ability it gives me to see exactly what we have and to be a good steward in utilizing the leftovers that are hidden in my refrigerator. Use your imagination as you come up with a food bar, with no recipes to follow, nothing is set in stone.

I have purchased some inexpensive clear glass bowls that I use to set up our food bars. Leftovers slapped out on the counter in an old margarine tub are not nearly as acceptable or inviting to our families as food carefully placed in individual containers. I know that changing containers makes a little more work, but I believe the enjoyment of our family makes it a worthwhile sacrifice.

May I offer you some encouragement regarding how you serve your lunches? Please, take the time to clear off your table. Too often, because we are so busy, lunch becomes the meal that is served amidst our papers, books, car trash, and dirty boy's socks! Taking just a few moments to clean off the table (even if you're just relocating the mess,) will provide a peaceful and non-distracting eating experience. Our children will elevate their standard of manners to the standard of the table... in other words; you get what you deserve if you feed them on a messy table! Also, please use napkins with your meal. Even a casual meal like lunch is a training time, so if you want your children to use napkins, provide them. If you're fine with them just wiping their mouths on their sleeves... Enough said?

I always include peanut butter and jelly as an alternative option on the food bar. Honestly though, it is a rare occasion when my children can't find something in the leftovers that they want to combine into a meal.

In our home, at breakfast and dinner, what you are served

is what you get to eat. When I set up a food bar, this is the one exception to the breakfast and dinner rule. I know that my children really enjoy the freedom of mixing and matching to make the lunch of their choice.

I *do not* offer cold cereal as a lunchtime choice. There is just not enough nutritional value in a bowl of cereal to keep my busy children going all afternoon. The fullness felt after a bowl of cereal will wear off quickly and I will be raising a family of continual snackers; not a healthy long-term goal. However, I do insist on a glass of milk at lunchtime and I encourage the children to add a piece of fruit to their plate along with whatever else they have chosen to eat. In addition, I make sure to provide some bread or rolls on our food bar.

Leftover Bar

This is the easiest bar to prepare. Simply empty the leftovers out of your refrigerator and pantry and place them into appropriate containers. Look over what you have to offer and place out any condiments that would help to complete the lunchtime offering. Don't hesitate to put out foods that don't seem to go together. Often, my children will come up with combinations of food that it would never have occurred to me to combine.

If what you have to offer seems inadequate, include a simple tossed salad. Nothing elaborate, just lettuce with some shredded carrot and chopped celery. Many leftovers will taste like a new and different meal altogether, when place over a salad. Encourage your children to try leftover meat and cold vegetables over lettuce and drizzled with their favorite salad dressing.

I usually have some type of leftover noodles in the refrigerator. Just as when placed on top of a salad, chopped meat and cold vegetables, reheated in the microwave, make a delicious lunch on top of a bed of leftover noodles. I keep a large shaker of Parmesan cheese on hand to sprinkle on top and this is the leftover lunch of choice for my youngest son Taylor.

MEXICAN BAR

Whenever I cook taco meat, I try to ensure that I cook enough to have leftover meat for a Mexican Bar lunch. Following are some suggestions for other foods to place out with the taco meat.

- Flour tortillas
- Corn chips
- Chopped lettuce (for taco salad or as a topping)
- Sour Cream
- Beans (pinto, black, kidney, or refried)
- Shredded cheese
- Black Olives
- Rice (to make burritos)
- Salsa
- Corn
- Diced Tomatoes

*No taco meat? Diced chicken tossed in salsa makes a good alternative to taco meat.

Baked Potato Bar

Baked potato bars are one of my children's favorite bar lunches. An hour before lunch, simply scrub and poke with a fork, the desired amount of potatoes. We prefer Russets. Bake at 400 degrees for one hour to get soft insides with a crispy skin. Here are some of our favorite toppings, but use what you have on hand!

- Shredded cheese
- Chopped broccoli
- Chili
- Sour Cream
- Bacon Bits
- BBQ chicken leftovers, diced
- Butter
- Plain yogurt
- Browned ground beef and cheese
- Pizza sauce and mozzarella
- Ranch Dressing

Really, the sky is the limit. I try to bake some extra potatoes to use the following morning for breakfast potatoes. Chopped up and sautéed with butter, green pepper, and onion, they are a great breakfast accompaniment.

SALAD BAR

Often with my potato bar, I put out a salad bar, as well. Fresh produce is the most often wasted food from my refrigerator. Setting up a weekly salad bar makes me more aware of what I have and more able to use those items before they spoil. Here are some ideas to get you thinking.

- Lettuce (mix what you have; i.e. iceberg, green leaf, romaine)
- Shredded cabbage, carrots
- Chopped onion, celery, green pepper
- Kidney beans
- Diced apple
- Orange segments
- Raisins
- Dried cranberries
- Leftover meats
- Broccoli, green beans, peas, corn, etc.
- Bacon bits
- Sunflower seeds

Salad bars are limited only by our imaginations, so be creative!

Pizza, Homemade Bread, and Stuffed Breads

These next lunch offerings are not as simple as the lunch bars, but with a little bit of effort, they provide a nutritious and really special lunch for your family.

Everyone in my family loves pizza. There are many ways to serve pizza for lunch and they range from as simple as an English muffin base, all of the way to your own homemade dough. Whatever base you choose, your children will be delighted with frequent pizza lunches.

Let me begin with some easy base and pizza topping ideas and then I will finish this chapter with an easy and delicious homemade dough and pizza sauce recipe.

Bases:
English Muffins, bagels, tortillas, hamburger buns, French bread

Toppings:
• Pepperoni
• Diced ham
• Pineapple
• Green peppers

- Onion
- Sweet peppers
- Sausage
- Ground Beef
- Tomatoes
- Pesto
- BBQ chicken, diced
- Black olives
- Diced broccoli

If you have it on hand, it can top a pizza! Be adventurous. My children especially enjoy the opportunity to top their own individual pizzas. Simply place the toppings out on the counter and let the children create to their heart's desire.

You will find many commercial brands of pizza topping, however they are much more expensive and no tastier than pizza sauce that you make yourself. Here is the recipe that my family always uses:

- 14 oz. can tomato sauce
- 1 TBS olive oil
- 1 tsp. each: oregano, basil, salt
- ½ tsp. garlic powder

I mix these ingredients right in the can and store leftovers in a plastic container.

For cheese I use a 2 to 1 mix of mozzarella to cheddar cheese. I always end with a sprinkle of Parmesan cheese on top of the pizza. The exception is a white pizza made with simply olive oil, garlic, and mozzarella cheese. (Occasionally I will add sliced tomatoes to this white pizza.

If you like your toppings to be a little crispy, place them on top of the cheese. For softer toppings, place them under the cheese with just one topping on the surface to identify the pizza type.

HOMEMADE PIZZA DOUGH

This is yummy! In a large bowl or mixer place:

- 2 c. warm water
- 2-Tbs. brown sugar
- 2-Tbs. yeast

Whisk together and let get bubbly, approximately 10 minutes.

Add:
- 2-Tbs. olive oil
- 1 ½ tsp. salt
- 5 c (approx) flour

- Mix well and then knead for 5 minutes. You can do this by hand or in a mixer. Just add flour until the mixer cleans the side of the bowl or until you cannot add more by hand and the dough is not sticky.
- Cover and let rise for 15 minutes. This makes two large pizzas.
- Bake at 450 degrees until golden and crispy. Although I own pizza stones, we prefer to use the inexpensive pizza screens, which allow the pizza to be crisp the whole way across the bottom.

SIMPLE HOMEMADE BREAD

Even the busiest mom should find the occasional spare moments to make some homemade bread. Fresh bread, straight from the oven, with honey or butter melting on it is a special treat that every child should enjoy at some point. Making bread isn't difficult; it just takes some practice. Come on; give it a whirl!

When I had three small children and no electric mixer, I used to make my homemade bread everyday during naptime. I had a predictable group of college boys that showed up everyday for fresh bread and "mom" conversation. Daily, we discussed classes, jobs, and future spouses over hot slices of delicious bread. That warm bread provided food for their hungry appetites and knowing that I would gladly serve it to them each day opened avenues for conversation that we might never have had otherwise.

Teach your children to bake bread. You will enjoy the time together and who knows, you might inspire a future baker. My oldest daughter had her own bread business when she was eleven years old. Her bread was delicious and she developed quite a clientele of faithful customers.

WHOLE WHEAT BREAD

1. Soften 1 TBS yeast in ¼ c warm water
2. In another bowl, combine:
   - 2 ½ c hot water
   - ½ c brown sugar
   - 3 tsp. salt
   - ¼ c shortening or vegetable oil
3. Cool this mixture to lukewarm
4. Stir in 3 c wheat flour and 1 c white flour. Mix well.
5. Add yeast mixture to flour mixture.
6. Add up to 4 c more white flour
7. If you are using a mixer, add flour until the dough hooks clean the side of the mixer. If mixing by hand, continue adding flour until you cannot incorporate any more flour.
8. Knead for 10 minutes.
9. Place in an oiled bowl and cover with a towel.
10. Let rise for 1 hour.
11. Punch down dough and shape into two loaves.
12. Place loaves in greased pans and cover. Allow to rise for 1 hour.
13. Bake at 375 degrees for 45 minutes. Cover with foil if tops brown too quickly.
14. Cool, out of pans, on wire racks. Butter tops while hot for a soft crust.

STUFFED BREADS

Let me share my secret for the simplest meal to feed your children on field trips, car trips, and family outings. Make a loaf of stuffed bread, grab paper plates and a bread knife, and be on your way. Stuffed bread is a sandwich in a loaf and makes for easy eating and virtually no cleanup. Stuffed bread can be made with any toppings you prefer, such as lunchmeat and cheese or pepperoni, mozzarella, and pizza sauce.

To make stuffed bread, use the previous recipe or purchase frozen bread dough from the grocery store. If using frozen dough, allow it to thaw in the refrigerator. At the point that you would form your dough into loaves, roll it out into an 8 by 12 rectangle. Brush the dough with the topping of your choice. With lunchmeat I generally use mustard, mayonnaise, and a little dill. Starting on an 8-inch end, layer three slices of meat and two slices of cheese. Roll the dough once, add another section of meat and cheese, and make another roll. Add one final section of meat and cheese. At this point you should only have enough dough to roll one last time. Roll the dough, tuck the ends under, and place seam-side down in a greased loaf pan. Allow loaves to rise for one hour. Bake at 375 degrees for 45 minutes. Allow loaves to cool before cutting. Buttering the tops while hot will make soft crusts.

SOUPS AND CHILI

Soups and chili are a great addition to your lunchtime repertoire. Although they take a bit of time to prepare, most soups can be made ahead of time and they will taste even better the day after they were made. Serve your soup with some bread, cornbread, biscuits, or muffins. Again, most of these can be made ahead and all you will have to do at lunchtime is reheat what you are serving. All of the following recipes serve 6-8.

Chili (good served with sour cream & cheddar cheese)

- Brown 2 lbs. of ground beef (We like our chili meaty!) with one chopped onion.
- Drain the beef and put it in a large pot with:
- 2 cans dark kidney beans, drained
- 1 can Mexican chilies and tomatoes
- 1 can diced tomatoes
- 1 large can tomato sauce
- 3 TBS chili powder (more to taste)
- 1 tsp. garlic powder

Bring to a boil and then lower heat to simmer for 2 hours.

Chicken Noodle Soup

- 3 tbsp olive oil
- 1 onion, large dice
- 3 carrots, peeled and cut in ½ inch pieces
- 2 celery ribs, cut in ½ inch pieces
- 4 sprigs of Thyme
- 1 bay leaf
- 1 ½ cups cooked, shredded chicken
- 2 quarts chicken stock (Recipe Below)
- 2 cups egg noodles
- Salt and pepper
- 1 handful chopped parsley

In a medium stockpot pour the olive oil and heat. Add in the onion, carrots, celery, thyme and bay, cook over medium heat until just softening. Pour in the stock and bring to a simmer. Add the egg noodles and simmer for about 6 more minutes. Add in the chicken, salt and pepper, and parsley. Bring to a full boil and turn off. This can be made ahead and saved for up to a week in the refrigerator or 3 months in the freezer.

Chicken Stock

- Bones from whole chicken
- 1 onion cut in 4 pieces
- 3 carrots cut in half
- 3 celery ribs cut in 3 pieces
- Water enough to cover
- 4 sprigs of Thyme
- 1 bay leaf

In a large stockpot place the chicken bones, onion, carrots, celery, thyme and bay. Cover completely with water and place over low heat. Allow simmer, never boiling, for 4-6 hours. Occasional skim the fat from the top of the water and stir. After 4-6 hours strain the stock into a container, use for soups, pasta or sauces. Can be stored in the refrigerator for up to 2 weeks or in the freezer for 3 months.

STEAK SOUP

In a large pot:
* Brown 1 lb. ground beef and 1 cup chopped onion

To the pot add:
* 3 cups frozen mixed vegetables
* 1 can stewed tomatoes, do not drain
* 2 cups water
* 1 cup sliced celery
* 1 beef bouillon cube
* ½ tsp pepper
* Bring to a boil.

Whisk together:
* 1 can beef broth
* ½ cup flour
* Add to beef mixture stirring constantly, return to boil.
* Reduce to simmer. Cover and simmer for 45 minutes.

This is particularly good on cold winter days. You can substitute leftover steak slices for the ground beef, as well.

CREAMED CABBAGE SOUP

(Trust me and try this, my kids absolutely LOVE it!)

- 2 cups chicken broth
- 1 onion, diced
- 1 c celery, diced
- 1 head cabbage, shredded (you can buy pre-shredded)
- 1 carrot, small dice
- ¼ c butter, cubed
- 3 TBS flour
- 1-cup milk
- 2 cups half and half
- 2 cups cubed cooked ham
- 1 ½ tsp salt
- ¼ tsp pepper
- ½ tsp thyme

Combine broth and vegetables, simmer 20 minutes or until vegetables are soft.

In a large saucepan, melt butter. Add flour to make a roux. Gradually add milk and cream, stir until thickened. Add vegetable mixture, ham, and spices. Heat through.

CHEESEBURGER SOUP

(My All-Time Most Requested Recipe)

- 1 lb. ground beef
- ¾ cup each: chopped onion, shredded carrots, diced celery
- 1 tsp. each: basil and parsley
- 4 TBS butter, divided
- 3 cups chicken broth
- 4 cups diced potatoes
- ¼ c flour
- 16 oz. Velveeta
- 1-½ cups milk
- ¾ tsp salt
- ¼ tsp pepper
- ½ c sour cream

In a large saucepan, brown beef and set aside. Wipe pan and sauté onion, carrots, celery, basil, and parsley, in 1 TBS butter. Add broth, potatoes, and beef. Bring to a boil. Reduce heat and simmer 20 minutes or until potatoes are cooked.

In a small skillet, melt 3 TBS butter; add flour to make a roux. Stir for 3 minutes. Add to soup and return soup to a boil. Cook for 2minutes. Return heat to low. Stir in cheese, milk, salt, and pepper. When cheese is melted, add sour cream.

Corn Chowder

- 1 lb bacon
- 1 onion, diced
- 8 potatoes, peeled, diced, and boiled until soft
- 6 cups milk
- 2 cups half and half
- 4 cans creamed corn
- 4 cans corn
- 2 TBS butter
- Salt and pepper to taste

Dice bacon and fry with onions. Drain fat.

Place bacon, onions, and all remaining ingredients, except for butter, in a large saucepan.

Bring slowly to a temperature that is just below a boil.

Reduce heat and simmer for ½ hour.

Before serving, put butter pats on top of soup and allow to melt.

This soup is rich and delicious! Even better the next day.

Italian Wedding Soup

Meatballs:
- 1 small onion, grated
- 1/3 cup chopped parsley
- 1 large egg
- 1 tsp minced garlic
- 1 tsp salt
- ¼ cup breadcrumbs
- ½ cup Parmesan cheese
- ½ pound ground beef
- ½ pound ground pork
- 1 tsp ground pepper

Soup:
- 12 cups chicken stock
- 6 cups spinach
- 2 cups couscous
- Salt and pepper

To make the meatballs, add all the ingredients in a mixing bowl and mix together thoroughly. Pinch off in little 1-inch rounds and roll until round and bake in a 400-degree oven for 10 minutes.

To make the soup, pour the stock into a large stockpot. Bring to a boil and add the meatballs and couscous. When the couscous is tender add in the spinach and salt and pepper. Bring to a boil and turn off. Sprinkle with Parmesan when ready to serve.

ROLLS AND BREADS TO ACCOMPANY YOUR LUNCH

The breads and rolls we choose to accompany our lunches do not always have to be as complicated as homemade bread. On the other hand, they do not have to be as simple and predictable as plain old white bread, either. Although, one of my husband's favorite childhood treats was Wonder Bread balls! Yuck, I don't recommend them! Before sharing some homemade recipes, let me recommend some easy alternatives.

Make use of the inexpensive, store-brand refrigerator rolls and biscuits. One of our favorite ways to use the refrigerated biscuits is to cut each biscuit into four pieces and then to dip the pieces into melted butter with various spices sprinkled into it. Bake these little tidbits in a 375-degree oven for approximately 15 minutes, watching closely to make sure they do not brown too much.

Warm flour tortillas make an excellent accompaniment to soups and salads, while cornbread is another warm bread choice. I use up leftover hamburger and hotdog rolls by buttering them, sprinkling them with Parmesan cheese, and toasting them under the broiler.

REFRIGERATOR ROLLS

- Mix together:
- 2 cups lukewarm water
- ½ cup sugar
- 1 ½ tsp salt
- 1 TBS yeast
- Stir well and add:
- 1 egg
- ¼ cup shortening
- 6 ½ -7 cups flour
- Stir well, but do not knead.

Place dough into a well greased bowl, cover with a towel, and place in the refrigerator.

When ready to use, shape dough into desired type of rolls and allow to rise, covered, for 1-½ hours.

Bake at 400 degrees for 12-15 minutes

Brush the tops of the rolls with butter while hot for a soft crust.

RAISED CRESCENTS

- 2 TBS yeast
- ¾ cup warm water
- ½ cup sugar
- ¼ cup plus 2 TBS butter, divided
- 2 TBS shortening
- 2 eggs
- 1 tsp salt
- 4-4 ½ cups flour

In a large mixing bowl, dissolve yeast in water. Add sugar, ¼ cup butter, shortening, eggs, salt, and 2 cups flour. Beat well. Add enough remaining flour to make a soft dough. Knead for 5 minutes.

Place in a greased bowl. Allow to rise, covered, for 1-½ hours.

Punch down dough and divide in half. Spread with remaining softened butter. Roll each half into a circle. Use a knife or pizza cutter to cut each circle into 12 pieces. Roll up wedges from the widest end and place point down on greased baking sheets.

Bake at 375 degrees for 8-10 minutes. Brush with additional butter while hot.

OATMEAL PAN BREAD

- 1-½ cups boiling water
- 1-cup oats
- 2 TBS yeast
- ½ cup warm water
- ¼ cup sugar
- 3 TBS butter, softened
- 2 tsp salt
- 1 egg, lightly beaten
- 4-4-¾ flour

In a small bowl, combine oats and boiling water.

Cool to lukewarm.
In a mixing bowl, dissolve yeast in warm water. Add sugar, butter, salt, egg, oat mixture, and 2 cups water.

Beat well. Add enough flour to make a soft dough. Knead until smooth.

Place in a greased bowl. Cover and let rise for 30 minutes. Punch dough down and press into a greased 9 by 13 pan. With a sharp knife cut a diamond pattern into the top of the bread.

Let rise until doubled.

Brush with 2 TBS melted butter and bake at 375 degrees for 15 minutes.

* Topping- mix together:
* 2 TBS grated Parmesan
* 1 tsp basil
* ½ tsp oregano
* ½-tsp garlic powder.

After 15 minutes of baking, brush bread with melted butter and sprinkle topping over the bread. Bake for 5 minutes. Cover with foil and bake for an additional five minutes.

To serve, tear diamond shape pieces off individually.

This bread is a favorite with my family and goes well with soups, all kinds of meats, and many Italian dishes. Make sure to grease your baking pan very well and cleanup will be a breeze!

CASSEROLE BATTER BREAD

(This is simple, non-shaped bread)

- 1 TBS yeast
- 1-¼ cups warm water
- 1 TBS sugar
- ½ tsp salt
- 2 ½ - 3 cups flour

In a large mixing bowl, dissolve yeast in water. Add sugar, salt, and 1 ½ cups water. Beat well. Add enough remaining flour to form a soft dough. Knead until smooth, approximately 6-8 minutes.

Place in a greased bowl and allow to rise, covered until doubled.

Punch down and place into a greased 1 qt. casserole dish. Cover and let rise till doubled.

With a sharp knife, make two slashes on the top of the bread.

Bake at 350 degrees for 40-45 minutes.

This is a great dough in which to add 1 TBS of your favorite spice. I especially like it as Dill Bread.

TEA TIME

This particular chapter of the book is also contained in my book, Rise and Shine. The sweetness of Tea Time fits both books! If you don't already own Rise and Shine, you can find it at www.characterhealth.com in the store.

Another great opportunity to read aloud to your children is during a time of the day that we call Tea Time. Tea Time can either be between breakfast and lunch or between lunch and dinner. This was not a regularly scheduled time, but instead is a break in our normal routine when we read aloud and enjoy some special treats.

Make the effort, (it won't require much) to make Tea Time a special time of the day. Sometimes, I purchased inexpensive, yet fun plates and napkins from the Dollar Store and we used these exclusively at Tea Time. Sometimes, the girls brought their dolls along to Tea Time and we set four extra places. Think creatively to find the ways that you can make Tea Time a memorable time for your children.

When you are preparing your grocery list, be sure to include the ingredients you will need for Tea Time. If you don't, Tea Time will never happen or it will be sadly disappointing. Better no Tea Time than a Tea Time that is lame, lame, Lame!

CREAMY GARLIC PASTA

- 1 box Penne Pasta
- 2 cloves garlic
- 2 tbsp butter
- 2 tbsp flour
- ¾ chicken broth or stock
- ¾ cup milk
- 2 tbsp basil
- 2 tsp oregano
- 1/3 cup grated Parmesan cheese
- Salt and Pepper to taste

Cook pasta in salted water until fork tender. In a medium saucepan melt the butter; add in the garlic and sauté for 1 minute. Add in the flour and whisk briskly. Pour in milk and broth and whisk until sauce thickens. Stir in basil, oregano, s/p, and cheese. Pour over the pasta and toss together.

Serve with warm crusty bread.

ASIAN BOWTIE PASTA

- 1 box bowtie pasta
- Sesame ginger salad dressing
- 1 red pepper
- ½ white onion
- 1 large handful snap peas
- Peanuts (optional)
- ½ bunch cilantro
- 2 cooked chicken breasts

Cook pasta until fork tender. Cool in the refrigerator. Small dice the red pepper, onion, and snap peas. Chop the cilantro very fine. Toss with the cooled pasta and sesame dressing. Cut the chicken into bite size pieces and toss with the pasta. Sprinkle with peanuts.

Pesto Pasta

- 1 large bunch of basil
- ¼ cup pine nuts
- ½ grated Parmesan cheese
- 1 clove garlic
- ½ -3/4 cup olive oil
- Salt and Pepper to taste
- Spaghetti Pasta- 1-inch handful per person

Cook pasta in salted water until al dente (tender to the bite). In a food processor or blender, blend together the basil, pine nuts, cheese, garlic and salt and pepper. Slowly pour in the olive oil. Toss half of the pesto with the spaghetti. Store the other half in the freezer until needed. Serve warm with crusty bread. Add chicken or tomatoes and mushrooms if desired.

BBQ Ribs

- 3 lbs Pork Spare-ribs
- Salt
- Pepper
- 1 tbsp Garlic powder
- 1 tsp Cayenne Pepper
- ¼ cup Worcestershire Sauce
- ¼ cup dark molasses
- 1 8oz jar of bbq sauce (I really enjoy honey bbq with this recipe)
- 1 large onion diced

Place the ribs on a cutting board and rub generously with salt, pepper, garlic, and cayenne. Feel free to use as much or as little of the seasonings as you like. The measurements are just a guideline. Put the ribs in the slow cooker with the Worcestershire, molasses and bbq. Dice the onion in a large dice. Sprinkle over the ribs. Cook on high for 4-5 hours, or on low over night.

Great served with baked potatoes or corn.

Honey Garlic Chicken

- 4 boneless skinless chicken thighs
- ½ cup ketchup
- ½ cup soy sauce
- 1/3-cup honey
- ¼ cup Worcestershire sauce
- 3 cloves garlic minced
- 1 large onion diced
- 4 carrots peeled and cut in 1 inch pieces

Dice the onion in a large dice and layer the bottom of the slow cooker with it. Next, peel and cut the carrot and layer it on top of the onion. Season the chicken thighs with salt and pepper and lay on top of the carrots. In a separate bowl, mix together the ketchup, soy sauce, honey, Worcestershire sauce, and garlic. Pour over the chicken, evenly. Cook at medium to high heat for 3 ½ hours. This is best served over white rice with a little soy sauce on the side for dipping. If you want to add a little heat to the dish you can mince up one Thai chili and add it to the sauce before cooking.

CHEESY CHICKEN AND RICE

- 4 boneless, skinless chicken breasts
- 1 large can cheddar cheese soup
- 2 cups rice
- 4 cups water

Cut the chicken breast into bite size pieces. Place in the slow cooker across the bottom as evenly as possible. Pour the cheddar cheese soup over the chicken and cook on high for 3 hours. The easiest way to make rice is in the microwave! In a large microwave safe bowl pour the rice and water, cook for about 15 minutes on medium high heat. Do not cover! Stir after 15 minutes and taste. The rice should be soft and fluffy, if it is still crunchy add ¼ cup more of water and cook for another 3 minutes. Serve the chicken over the rice with plenty of the soup. We love this for a Sunday lunch after church.

www.characterhealth.com

Cookies

Classic Chocolate Chip

- 2 sticks butter, softened
- ¾ cups white sugar
- ¾ cups packed brown sugar (Seriously pack as much as you can!)
- 2 large eggs
- 2 tsp vanilla extract (or almond extract if you feel adventurous)
- 2 ¼ cup all purpose flour
- 1 tsp baking soda
- ½ tsp salt
- 1 tsp cinnamon
- 2 cups semi sweet chocolate chips

In a mixing bowl cream together the sugars and the butter. This will take about 3 minutes and the mixture should look pale in color and creamy. Add in the eggs and the extract. Beat on medium speed for another 3 minutes. Again, it should look pale and fluffy this time. Add in the dry ingredients. The way I do it is add in the baking soda, salt, cinnamon and one cup of the flour. Mix until smooth then add in the rest of the flour and mix again. Stir in the chocolate chips by hand. Drop by spoonfuls onto a parchment lined baking pan. Bake in a preheated

350-degree oven for 8 minutes. Let cool on the pan for one minute then remove to a wire cooling rack and cool completely. Yields 3 dozen.

SOFT MOLASSES COOKIES

- ¾ cup butter, melted
- 1 cup white sugar
- 1 large egg
- 1/3-cup dark molasses
- 2-½ cups all-purpose flour
- 2 tsp baking soda
- ½ tsp salt
- 1 tsp cinnamon
- ½ tsp ginger
- ½ tsp cloves
- ½ cup sugar

In a mixing bowl cream together the butter, sugar, molasses and egg. In a separate bowl mix the dry ingredients. Slowly add the flour mixture into the mixing bowl 1 cup at a time. Make sure to scrape the sides of the bowl periodically. After everything is combined let the dough chill in the refrigerator for 1 hour. Preheat the oven to 350. After the dough is chilled, start rolling into 1-inch size rounds. Roll in the ½ cup of sugar and bake for 7 minutes. The cookies will appear light brown and cracked when finished. Yields 3 ½ dozen

Vanilla Sugar Cookies

- 1 cup butter, softened (2 sticks)
- 1 ½ cup sugar
- 2 eggs
- 2 tsp vanilla extract
- 2 ¾ cups flour
- 2 tsp cream of tartar
- 1 tsp baking soda
- ½ tsp salt
- ½ cup sugar for rolling

In a mixing bowl cream the butter and sugar. It will be light in color and airy. Scrape the sides of the bowl. Add in the eggs and vanilla. Beat together on medium speed for about 3 minutes. Scrape the sides of the bowl again. In a separate bowl combine the dry ingredients. Slowly add to the mixing bowl. Let chill in the refrigerator for about 1 hour. Preheat the oven to 325. Take the chilled dough and make 1-inch rounds. Roll in the extra sugar. Bake for about 8 minutes. The cookies will be cracked and light golden when finished. Cool completely on a metal rack. Yields 4 ½ dozen.

Chocolate Peppermint Cookies

- ½ cup of butter, softened
- ¾ cups white sugar
- 1 egg
- ¼ tsp peppermint extract
- 1-¼ cups all-purpose flour
- 1/3 cup cocoa powder
- ½ tsp salt
- ½ baking soda
- ¼ baking powder
- 1 candy cane, finely crushed
- 1/3-cup semi-sweet chocolate chips.

In a mixing bowl cream the butter and sugar until light and airy. Scrape the bowl and add in the egg and peppermint. Beat for 3 minutes on medium speed. In a separate bowl combine the flour, cocoa, baking soda, and baking powder. Add into the mixing bowl one cup at a time. Scrape down the sides of the bowl occasionally. Add in the chocolate chips. Preheat the oven to 325. Scoop the dough by rounded spoonfuls on to a parchment lined baking sheet. Bake for 10 minutes. Remove from the oven and immediately sprinkle with the crushed candy cane. Let cool on a metal rack. Yields 4 dozen

Peanut Butter Kisses

- ½ cup shortening
- ¾ cup peanut butter
- 1/3 cup white sugar
- 1/3 cup packed light brown sugar
- 1 large egg
- 2 tbsp whole milk
- 1 tsp vanilla extract
- 1-½ cups all-purpose flour
- 1 tsp baking soda
- ½ tsp salt
- 1 bag Hershey's Kisses

In a mixing bowl cream together the shortening, peanut butter, and sugars. Mixture should be pale in color and airy when done. Add in the egg, milk and vanilla and beat on medium speed for about 3 minutes. Scrape down the sides of the bowl. In a separate bowl combine the flour, baking soda and salt. Slowly add to the mixing bowl 1 cup at a time. After the flour is completely added let stand for about 10 minutes. Drop by rounded spoonfuls onto a parchment lined baking sheet.

Bake for 7 minutes in a 325-degree oven. Remove from the oven and place a Hershey's kiss in the center of the cookie. Return to the oven and bake for 3 more minutes. Cool completely on a metal rack. Yields 3 dozen

Tea Time

Tea Time

Another great opportunity to read aloud to your children is during a time of the day that we called Tea Time. Tea Time can either be between breakfast and lunch or between lunch and dinner. This was not a regularly scheduled time, but instead was a break in our normal routine when we would read aloud and enjoy some special treats. Allow me to share some of our favorite Tea Time recipes.

Muddy Buddies

- 9 cups Crispix
- 1 cup chocolate chips
- ½ cup peanut butter
- ¼ cup butter
- 1 tsp vanilla
- 1-½ cups powdered sugar

Melt chips, peanut butter and butter in the microwave. Stir in the vanilla.

Pour over cereal and stir well.

Place in a large bag with powdered sugar. Shake the bag vigorously. Spread on wax paper to cool.

CARAMEL CORN

- 2 cups brown sugar
- 1-cup butter
- ½ cup light corn syrup
- 1 tsp salt
- ½ tsp baking soda
- 5 Qts. popped corn (1 ½ cups unpopped)

Keep popcorn in a 200-degree oven while making syrup.

Over low heat, combine brown sugar, syrup, butter, and salt.

Bring to a boil and boil for 5 minutes, stirring constantly.

Remove from heat and stir in baking soda.

Pour over popcorn (divided into several rimmed cookie sheets). Stir to coat.

Bake at 250 degrees for one hour, stirring every 15 minutes.

Cool on wax paper.

Store in a tightly sealed container.

G.O.R.P. (GOOD OL' RAISINS AND PEANUTS)

- 2 cups cheerios
- 1-cup raisins
- 1-cup peanuts
- ½ cup M&Ms

This recipe is meant to be mixed up! Have your toddler help measure out the ingredients and add anything to it that sounds good! Some suggestions are: dried cranberries, mini marshmallows, walnuts, or honey grahams.

Bagel Chips

- 2 cinnamon swirl bagels
- 2 tbsp melted butter
- Cinnamon sugar mix

Stand the bagels on their ends and slice very thin. Lay them out on a sheet pan, spread with the melted butter and sprinkle with cinnamon sugar. Bake at 350 for 10-15 minutes, until golden brown and crispy.

Serve with peanut butter for dipping.

Cinnamon Heart Popcorn

- 1-cup butter
- ½ cup corn syrup
- 1 ½ cups cinnamon red hearts
- 8 cups popped popcorn

Melt the butter, cinnamon heart and corn syrup together. Mix with popcorn and spread out on a parchment lined baking sheet. Bake at 250 until candy coating is set, about 30 minutes. Cool and enjoy!

CHEX MIX

- 3 cups rice Chex cereal
- 2 cups mini pretzels
- 1-cup cashews
- 1-cup cheddar crackers
- ¾ cups grated Parmesan cheese
- ½ stick butter
- Pinch of garlic powder

Mix all the ingredients together and spread on a baking sheet. Bake at 350 for 10 minutes. Stir once while baking.

BANANA SNACK CAKE

- 1-cup sugar
- 2 eggs
- 1tsp vanilla
- 2 cups flour
- 1 ½ tsp baking soda
- 1 c butter
- ½ cup butter or sour milk (put 1 tsp vinegar in bottom of ½ measuring cup, fill to top with milk)
- 1-cup (2 medium) bananas, mashed
- 1-cup quick-cooking oatmeal
- ½ tsp salt
- 1 cup chocolate chips

Cream butter, sugar, and eggs together.

Stir in milk, bananas, and vanilla, mixing well.

Stir in flour, oats, soda, and salt.

Stir in chips.

Pour into a greased 9 by 13 pan. Bake at 350 degrees for 30-35 minutes or until a cake tester comes out clean.

* Individual servings of this cake freeze well.

GORILLA BREAD

- ½-cup sugar
- 3 tsp cinnamon
- ½ cup butter
- 1 cup brown sugar, packed
- 8 oz. cream cheese
- 2-12 oz. cans refrigerated biscuits
- 1 ½ cup chopped nuts

Spray a Bundt pan.

Mix white sugar and cinnamon

Melt butter and brown sugar over low heat, set aside

Cut cream cheese into 20 cubes

Flatten biscuits and sprinkle with ½ tsp of cinnamon/sugar

Wrap each biscuit around cream cheese cube

Sprinkle ½ cup nuts into pan

Place ½ of biscuits into pan

Sprinkle with cinnamon/sugar

Pour ½ of melted butter over biscuits

Sprinkle ½ cup nuts

Layer remaining biscuits, cinnamon/sugar, and butter

Sprinkle with remaining nuts

Bake at 350 for 30 minutes. Cool 5 minutes. Place plate on top and invert

Strawberry Yogurt Dip

- 1 ½ cups frozen strawberries, thawed
- 8 oz. strawberry yogurt
- 1 cup whipped topping

In a bowl, mash the berries. Add yogurt and stir to mix well. Fold in whipped topping. Serve with fruit or angel food cake cubes.

Fruit Kabob suggestions:
- Honeydew
- Cantaloupe
- Watermelon
- Strawberries
- Chopped peaches
- Halved grapes
- Kiwi slices
- Orange segments
- Banana coins
- Pineapple

Any of these, served on a toothpick, make a fun Tea Time treat!

Contact Us

Steve and Megan Scheibner travel extensively facilitating parenting, marriage, and men's and women's conferences for churches and other organizations.

Conferences Available Include:
- Parenting Matters
  Marriage Matters
  Character Matters
  Second Mile Leadership for Men
- When God Writes Your Story
  The Wise Wife
  The A-Z of a Character Healthy Homeschool
- The Discipling Mom
- and more....

To speak with Steve or Megan please call:

1-877-577-2736 or, send them an email by clicking the Contact Us tab at:

Characterhealth.com

also, follow them on twitter:
@SteveScheibner
@Meganscheibner
@CharacterHealth

OTHER BOOKS BY MEGAN ANN SCHEIBNER:

In My Seat:
A Pilot's Story from Sept. 10th–11th

Grand Slam:
An Athletes Guide to Success in Life

Rise and Shine:
Routines and Recipes For Your Morning

Lunch and Literature

Dinner and Discipleship

Studies in Character

An A to Z Guide For Characterhealthy Homeschooling

Other Books by Steve Scheibner:

Bible Basics (Now available with a DVD for small group studies)

Books by Steve and Megan Scheibner:

Eight Rules of Communication For Successful Marriages

Studies in Character

The King of Thing and the Kingdom of Thingdom

www.characterhealth.com

DVD Series Available:

Parenting Matters:
The Nine Practices of the Pro-Active Parent

Character Matters:
The Nine Practices of Character Healthy Youth

The Toddler Toolbox

Battling With Behavior

Bible Basics

Subscribe to Steve and Megan's blogs:

- *www.SteveScheibner.com*
- *www.MeganScheibner.com*

You can find these books and other resources at:

www.characterhealth.com

BIOGRAPHY OF MEGAN SCHEIBNER

Megan was born March 13th 1962 and came home to her adoptive family March 15th. She grew up in York, PA and graduated from York Suburban H.S. in 1980. Four years later, she earned a B.A. in Speech Communications from West Chester University. She uses her degree as she teaches and speaks at conferences and women's ministry functions, as well as in individual and couples counseling.

Megan is the home schooling mother of eight beautiful children, four boys and four girls. She has been married for 29 years to her college sweetheart, Steve Scheibner. Together they have co-authored Parenting Matters, The Nine

Practices of the Pro-Active Parent. She is also the author of a series of discipleship books for mothers and several devotional Bible studies. She authored, "In My Seat," the story of Steve's 9/11 experience, that has captivated millions on YouTube. Her newest book, "An A-Z Guide For Character-Healthy Homeschooling" provides encouragement and practical tips gained through her 20 plus years of homeschooling experience. She is a popular speaker, guest on Family Talk with Dr. James Dobson, and TV personality on the Glenn Beck TV show.

Megan and her husband Steve share a strong desire to equip today's parents to raise the next generation of character healthy leaders. In her spare time, she loves to run and play tennis. Megan enjoys writing, cooking, feeding teenagers, reading, and everything pertaining to the Boston Red Sox.

Books by Megan:

- Character Matters: A Daily Step-By-Step Guide To Developing Courageous Character
- Eight Rules of Communication For Successful Marriages
- An A-Z Guide For Character-Healthy Homeschooling
- In My Seat: A Pilot's Story From Sept.10th-11th.
- Grand Slam: A Four Week Devotional Bible Study For Christian Athletes.
- Rise and Shine: Recipes and Routines For Your Morning.
- Lunch and Literature.
- Dinner and Discipleship.
- Studies in Character.
- The King of Thing and The Kingdom of Thingdom.

NOTES:

NOTES:

....
....
....
....
....
....
....
....
....
....
....
....
....
....
....

NOTES:

NOTES:

NOTES:

www.characterhealth.com